LILY O'CONNOR

Can Lily O'Shea come out to play?

A Brandon Original Paperback

Published in 2000 by Brandon
an imprint of Mount Eagle Publications
Dingle, Co. Kerry, Ireland

10 9 8 7 6 5 4 3 2 1

ISBN 0 86322 267 6
(original paperback)

Cover design: id communications, Tralee
Typesetting: Red Barn Publishing, Skeagh, Skibbereen
Printed by Colourbooks Ltd, Ireland.

Can Lily O'Shea Come Out to Play?

For Mammy

CONTENTS

Part 2: Cabra, Benburb Street and Cabra West

INTRODUCTION

Lily O'Connor's book is a remarkable achievement. It consists of a series of vignettes, recording life in the poorer areas of Dublin city, in the thirties, forties and fifties. It is simply written with a sharp eye for description and detail and a remarkable and accurate ear for dialogue. Like James Joyce, an artist in exile, she too has forgotten nothing of her native city.

Ms O'Connor charts a world that is largely gone. There is less poverty in Dublin, although there are still slums, and there are now new and more desperate problems with which the urban poor have to cope, especially the scourge of drugs and the turf wars of drug barons. In the world described in this book there is still one powerful asset for the disadvantaged – the sense of community in which neighbours would rally round in an emergency. This neighbourliness stretched right across the sectarian divide, a fact very important in the lives of those like the O'Sheas, who were from a family of mixed religious background.

One of the constant themes of the book is a tug-of-war between the Church of Ireland and the Roman Catholic Church for possession of the right to educate the children and ultimately bring them up according to the rights of a particular Christian sect.

Lily's mother, one of the patient, self-sacrificing, hard-working women depicted so clearly in the plays of Sean O'Casey, struggled desperately against the odds to bring up her family. Her father, charming, shiftless and often drunk, could have emerged from the pages of D.H. Lawrence or Frank O'Connor, for there is something universal about this kind of working-class father. If anything the scenes depicted are closer to the world of Frank O'Connor, with its threat of drink, the pawnshop and disease. One thinks of O'Connor's poignant phrase put into the mouth of his character, Larry Delaney, "I could never get over the lonesomeness of the kitchen without the clock," after the clock had been pawned to provide the father with drink.

Many of the inner city communities have now been broken up with disastrous social results. The O'Sheas were part of this process, moving out to the new working-class suburb of Cabra and then, lonely for the old life, back into the city to even less satisfactory accommodation. Lily O'Connor captures, with the patient memory of the exile, a forgotten world. Evocative smells are conjured up: the human, sometimes overpowering, smell of its tenements, the clean perfumed wafts from the wife of the Protestant minister, the smell of a slop bucket.

Although it was a world of deprivation, both loyalty and courage were displayed. One striking moment is when Lily's mother refuses to boycott an unfortunate neighbour who has had a child out of wedlock. It was a cruel and judgemental world then, and this neighbour was subsequently evicted, for daring to flout the conventions.

This book will carry memories for those who know Dublin and remember it as it was forty or fifty years ago. But its warmth and wisdom are accessible not just to native Dubliners – its themes are universal and will be recognised by city dwellers all over the world. Thanks to the talent of Lily O'Connor we are privileged to have a glimpse into a world that has now vanished in the company of a humane and engaging writer.

Senator David Norris

PART 1:
THE TENEMENTS

35 Fitzgibbon Street

Down on her knees scrubbing the floorboards in a tenement room, Mammy suddenly remembered it was her twenty-first birthday. She had been married two years and had two young children.

Alice Crawte could never have known what sort of a life she was letting herself in for when she married John O'Shea, a charming, carefree Catholic. They married in her church, a Protestant church, and moved in with his family, but living in a home with practising Catholics led to problems – especially when a baby arrived.

"Under the eyes of the Catholic Church, youse are not married," the O'Shea family reminded them constantly.

After much searching, they found a front room on the ground floor of a four-storey tenement house in Fitzgibbon Street. These old, dilapidated Georgian houses were the only accommodation available to poor families in the 1930s.

The door of our room was to the left of a large dark hall. It was a big room. Heavy shutters, folded on hinges, were pushed well back from a long, narrow window. I slept with my three sisters in a bed on one side of this window. My two brothers, Robbie and Johnny, slept in a small bed on the opposite side.

Lying in bed at night, I'd swear I could see strange faces in the dim corners of the high ornate ceiling above me. But I'd feel comforted when I'd sit up, look over at the fireplace and see Mammy sitting there. The gas globe would be lowered. She'd be combing her thick black hair and pinning it back up again. Her pale face would be glowing as she'd sing to us quietly. Her apron would be lying over a chair. Two China collie dogs sat on our high wooden mantelpiece, one on each end, staring in the same direction, towards Mammy and Daddy's big bed down the far end of the room.

A small iron gas cooker was stuck in a dark recess next to the fire. Mammy seldom had enough pennies to light it. We didn't have much, just the bare necessities: a well-scrubbed wooden table surrounded by kitchen chairs, a wobbly brown dresser and an old wardrobe, propped up on one side with cardboard. Everything else was either hanging on the back of the door, stuffed under our beds or in corners.

Granny Crawte moved in with us when my grandfather left her for another woman. She lived in the small back room that led off ours. Mammy never allowed us to go into her room unless invited.

"Come away from Granny's door," she'd call out when we'd fiddle with its loose brass knob.

Granny's little room looked out into the yard, lavatory and clothes line. She would be so grateful when Daddy would clean her window, but wished he wouldn't keep asking, "How's yer window, Mum?" for weeks after.

At night we'd hear scurrying and scratching in the basement below us. Unlike in a lot of other tenements, no one lived in our basement – except rats. It was a dump for old fibre mattresses and rusty iron bed springs.

A black iron railings protected us children from the filthy area beneath our window. Mothers tied their babies' prams to these railings while they got on with their housework. The babies sucked their dummies or crusts contentedly.

When I was one year old and Annie a new baby, Mammy would put the two of us in our old brown pram and tie it to the front railings. A lady would often stop and talk to me. One day she gave me a bunch of marigolds. When Mammy looked out the window and saw me feeding Annie with them, she rushed out, wiped the petals from her mouth and grabbed the bare stalks from me. From then on, I was out of the pram and played around the main hall door, sitting on the iron footscraper or struggling up and down the stone steps with Jumbo, my wooden elephant. Other times, I held on to our pram watching my big brother and sister, Robbie and Kathleen, playing on the footpath.

The lavatory was in our small backyard, which was enclosed by a high brick wall. It was for the use of the entire house, four or five large families. Whenever I wanted to use it, I would run in from the street shouting, "Mammy, I want to do me sometin'! Can I have a bit a' paper?"

Mammy'd tear off a scrap of newspaper, crumple it and rub it vigorously to make it soft. Sometimes a man would be in the lavatory with the big rusty bolt pulled across. I'd have to knock and wait till he finished reading his newspaper.

Living on the ground floor, Daddy was responsible for keeping the yard clean. Standing with the other children of the house, I would watch him throw one bucket after another of Jeyes Fluid and water into the lavatory. I can still smell that strong disinfectant and see the milky liquid flowing out into the yard towards our feet.

"Is that yer daddy?" the other children would ask as he swept it down the small drain.

I'd nod proudly.

At night the stairs were areas of pitch blackness, and, as the main hall door would be often left open, anyone could wander in and sleep behind it. Sometimes we'd be holding ourselves, wanting to go to the lavatory but too afraid to go out to the dark yard on our own.

"Go in the bucket. God knows who's out there," Mammy would say quietly, when she saw us peeping into the hall.

Each morning the women would struggle down with their slop buckets to empty. Whenever Daddy was around, he'd take it off them.

"Here, give me that bucket, for God's sake; I'll empty it for ya," he'd say, tricking around with them.

"T'anks, John, God bless ya," they'd say, straightening up.

14

There was a small fan-like window over the main hall door. When the door was closed over, light filtered through from a lamp-post outside, casting eerie shadows into the hall. If we were bold in bed and kept pushing each other, Mammy would threaten us.

"I'll put youse all outside in the dark hall with the bogey-man and close the door!" she'd say crossly.

Mammy knew everyone's footsteps passing through the hall.

"There's Luke on his way home from work," she'd say quietly.

Luke lived with his brother in a tiny room at the top of our house. Whenever he saw me, he'd smile and pat my head with his newspaper.

"How come ya haven't got yer mammy's black hair like yer sisters?" he'd joke. "You look like yer awl fella."

Someone would give the main hall door a good hard push, closing it.

"There's Missus Murphy coming back from confession," Mammy would whisper.

A bump against our door at night would make us all jump.

"It's only Mister Murphy," Mammy would say. "He's drunk again. Sounds like someone is helping him up the stairs."

We would wait to hear Mrs Murphy's loud voice above us: "Where de hell have ya been?"

Mr Murphy, a seaman, was once washed overboard and nearly drowned, but a wave swept him back up on board again. Sometimes in her fit of temper, Mrs Murphy would let him have it.

"Even de sea wouldn't have ya, it t'rew ya back!" she'd shout.

GETTING READY FOR SUNDAY

Sunday was a special day, and all the mothers worked hard on Saturday preparing for it. Rooms were thoroughly cleaned, and each neighbour swept or scrubbed her own flight of stairs. That was an unspoken rule in the tenements, and God help the woman who didn't do hers.

"~~Jesus~~, she's very dirty," they'd say behind her back.

We did our bit. I would sprinkle wet tea leaves on the bare boards in the hall to keep down the dust while Mammy swept it out on to the path. But the tea leaves couldn't get rid of the smell of baby sick that lingered in the hall when a pram had been left there overnight.

Clothes had to be washed. Mammy was lucky; she could use the line in the yard. On the upper floors, the women dried their washing by hanging it on a line pushed out of a back window with a pole. The dusty windowsills would be scrubbed, so as not to dirty the washing as it flapped back.

Throughout the day, pawnshops would be packed with women pushing their way to the counter to redeem their husbands' suits for mass next morning. These suits would be back in the pawn first thing Monday.

"It's a good day when ya have sometin' t'pawn," Mrs Murphy would often say to Mammy, as she'd pass through our hall with a bundle.

After the rooms were cleaned, mothers would pull up their windows, lean out and shout down to their children, "Come up for yer baths, the lot of youse, before I go down and murder youse!"

Saturday night was bath night. A small tin bath would be placed in front of our big smoky fire. Mammy would have dampened the turf to make it go further. Our clergyman, Mr Campbell, had turf or coal delivered to us every week. I'd feel important when I'd hear the coal man shout out our name in the hall.

"O'Shea! One bag a' turf for O'Shea!"

Mammy would rush to the door and show him in. Neighbours looked on enviously, but later on she'd hear them say, "I'd rather be a Catholic than have free turf."

Having stacked up the fire, Mammy would carry in a large pot of water from the yard and plonk it down on the smoking turf. We'd all be washed in the same water with Lifebouy soup. After we were dried, we'd sit in front of the fire in our clean vests and knickers toasting bread. Our dirty clothes would then be washed in the soapy bath water.

Annie and I would long for our hair to be curled up in ringlets.

"Can you curl our hair up with rags, Mammy, for Sunday? Please, like everyone else has!"

Daddy came home drunk one Saturday night. He roared with laughter when he saw Annie's black hair curled up in little white rags, the ends all hanging around her face.

"Will ya look at the state of Annie; for Jaysus sake, she looks like a bleeding lampshade!"

Sunday morning chapel bells would be ringing, calling everyone to mass. Mammy would be on her knees cleaning out the fire. Robbie, our big brother, would be getting ready to go to St George's Church to pump the organ for sixpence. Daddy would be snoring under the blankets fast asleep – he was not an early riser. My sisters and I would stand at the window watching for Miss Munro, our Sunday school teacher, to take us to church. We'd tap the window to our pals as they passed by with their whole families, even their daddies, with them, all going to mass wearing their best Sunday clothes. We'd have our clean clothes on too. Once when Mammy didn't have a pair of socks for Sylvia, Kathleen stayed in all day Saturday and knitted her a pair out of odd bits of wool.

By midday, mothers would be back in their aprons queuing up to wash their cabbages at the tap in the yard. Soon the smell of corned beef, cabbage and potatoes would drift from under every door as Sunday dinner was being cooked.

SUNDAY SCHOOL

Miss Munro would knock gently on our door. Mammy would only barely open it. She didn't want Miss Munro to see Daddy in bed or, worse still, the slop bucket not emptied.

"Are they ready, Mrs O'Shea?" Miss Munro would say, smiling as she peeped around the door.

Miss Munro came every week to take the five of us to Sunday school. Mammy went to church on her own in the evening. I looked forward to seeing her. This tall, slim, reserved lady lived with her parents in a small house near the Royal Canal. She would hold little Sylvia's hand as we cut up Charles Lane, or the Barrack Lane as we children called it, to our small Protestant church, the Free Church in Charles Street. My big sister Kathleen would drag Johnny along, while Annie and I skipped together.

Before service, we would sit in a group at the back. Miss Munro would hand around a small picture to each one of us. The picture of Daniel in the lion's den held me in awe. I thought of the huge lions in Dublin Zoo, locked up in small cages, roaring to be fed. I wondered if God would close their mouths if they escaped!

One week we were each given a text with a line from the Bible printed on it. Mine had the words "Walk to Please

God" in large gold letters. Mammy tacked it on the wall over my part of the bed.

After Sunday school, we sat on the cushioned seats beside the grown-up people. These posh parishioners believed in helping their own. They'd pass on their addresses to Mr Campbell for parcels of old clothes to be picked up by the poor of the parish.

While Mr Campbell was preaching his sermon, we'd dream and gaze around at all the colourful pictures in the windows.

Harvest Sunday was great. Fruit and bunches of golden wheat would be displayed around the seats of the church, and our favourite hymn, "All Things Bright and Beautiful", would be sung. Kneeling down, our mouths watered at the smell of the big shiny red apples that lay temptingly in front of us along the tops of the pews.

"You mustn't lick the apples," we'd say quietly to Johnny, grabbing the apples from him. We never knew where the fruit went.

Our service and Sunday school took over an hour. Mr Campbell would be standing at the door of his church shaking hands with the people as they left. We always had to make sure he'd seen us.

"Did Mister Campbell see youse?" Mammy would be sure to ask when we'd arrive home.

"Yes, he did," we'd all answer, and so did the Catholic children in Charles Street. They ran after us shouting, "Proddy woddy on the wall, half a loaf will do them all!"

NEIGHBOURS HELPED EACH OTHER

Living in such cramped conditions, neighbours often had arguments and would totally ignore each other. As we were a Protestant family living in a Catholic community, we had to be extra careful.

Mammy flew into a panic one day when I came racing into our room bursting with the latest news.

"Mammy, do you know whose daddy is in the IRA? And do you know what he did?"

Mammy glared at me: "Shh...."

Dropping the blanket she was examining, she quickly rushed to the door of our room and banged it closed. I knew then to lower my voice, for I had forgotten that even the walls had ears.

"And after he did it," I quickly whispered, "Mister Murphy ran home and hid under the bed."

Bending over the table, Mammy began preparing our tea, cutting slice after slice of bread.

"Children, my God, they'd hang you," she sighed.

But when a crisis occurred, religious differences, jealousies and grudges would soon be forgotten. Neighbours would be there to help all they possibly could.

When I scalded my feet and couldn't walk, a neighbour lifted her baby out of her pram and loaned it to Mammy to wheel me daily to the children's hospital for clean dressings.

"How can I thank you?" Mammy asked her.

"Just say a prayer for me," she answered.

Mammy would also help them when she could. She thought nothing of standing in a soup queue in the cold for hours to take back a bowl of hot soup to a neighbour. This neighbour, like a lot of Dublin people, was too proud to be seen standing in this queue.

"God bless you, I'll remember you in my prayers," she'd say gratefully, grabbing the bowl of hot soup from Mammy.

And help came when it was needed urgently from the most unexpected person. One day I was out in the street playing with Kathleen and Annie. Kathleen picked up a lighted cigarette butt from the kerb and blew the red-hot ash to keep it alight. Tricking around, I pushed Kathleen's hand, and the red-hot ash went straight into Annie's eye. Kathleen led her home screaming with pain. I ran ahead. Our milkman, Ray, was standing at the door of our room with his milk churn. He came twice a day, morning and afternoon, on his horse and cart. He'd always have time for a chat. Mammy had her jug in her hand waiting for it to be filled.

"~~Jesus~~," she cried when I told her what happened.

Ray didn't waste time. He dropped the milk churn, grabbed Annie, held back her head and licked every bit of ash out of her eye.

"Just say a prayer for me," he called back when Mammy tried to thank him.

GRANNY

"He's dying, Ellen, and he's calling for you. Please come back with me," the woman at our door begged Granny.

Granny was a proud woman and could not forgive Granddad for being unfaithful – not even on his deathbed.

Neighbours passing through the hall would see a small, straight, elderly woman coming out of her door. Granny Crawte would be off to the backyard to fill her kettle. Her grey hair was swept well back from her pale, smooth skin and pinned up tight in a bun. Unlike the other women, she wore no apron over her long dark skirt that covered her soft black laced-up boots.

"There goes the English lady, Missus Crawte," they'd whisper.

Granny put up with no nonsense. After hearing me pestering Mammy for a ha'penny one evening, she rushed out of her room, grabbed hold of my arm and pushed me into the dark shadowy hall. The large key clicked loudly in our big black lock. I tried to turn the handle and kicked against the door.

"I hate you, Granny! I wish you were dead!" I sobbed.

After a few minutes Mammy let me in.

"Be good now," she said, wiping my face with the wet corner of a towel. Putting her hand in her apron picket, she found a sweet for me. It tasted of tobacco from the Woodbine butt that she kept in there.

"Granny said you can go into her room and look at her cards. Now go on, and don't bump into her sore leg."

Whenever we were good, Granny would allow us to go into her little room. I would forget that she had ulcers on her legs and couldn't help bumping against her. I liked being with her on my own and would stare curiously around. There was a Fry's Cocoa tin on one end of her mantelpiece full of small glass golliwogs. It was Robbie's. The golliwogs had come free with her cocoa, and she had collected them for him.

"Can I listen to the tide coming in?" I'd say, picking up a large pink seashell and holding it up to my ear.

A red oil lamp stood on the other end of her mantelpiece. Beside it was her cream-coloured bone matchbox cover with a picture of Lord Kitchener on it. Granny's box of matches were slid inside. Granny would wait until it was almost dark before she lit her lamp. She'd turn its wick up slowly, letting the globe warm first. The glow from her lamp would throw a shadow over her single bed. With the fire flickering and her flowered curtains pulled across, the room was warm and homely. I'd sit down at her table when I'd see her drag out her big black trunk from under her bed. Her name, Ellen Mary Crawte, was printed in large letters on the lid. She had brought this trunk with her from England. I wasn't allowed go near it. All her private things were kept in there. Lifting up its squeaky lid, she'd let it drop back gently. Out would come what I was waiting for: several old-fashioned chocolate boxes crammed full of beautiful cards which had been sent to her over the years. Granny would sit down and pick up her sewing while I sorted out my favourites, the ones with the delicate lace on the front. Some had "To My Dear Mother" embroidered on them.

"They're from your Uncle Al," she'd say, handing me her needle to thread.

Granny was never idle. She'd mend all our clothes and her own. She had once been a lady-in-waiting in England – well, that's what Mammy always said – and was good with a needle and thread. At the first sign of winter, she would make camphor bags for each one of us.

"Don't take it off now. It will keep you from catching cold," she'd say, tying the little muslin bag around my neck.

I kept my camphor bag on all through the winter.

"Smell me camphor bag that me granny made me," I'd say, showing off to Mary Murphy who lived in our house.

Mary would pull down the neck of her jersey.

"Well, look at what me granny gave me. She gave me a medal that's blessed. She even pinned it to me vest, so she did!"

Granny also made us hankies by hand out of old sheets that couldn't be patched any more. She would pin them to our jerseys before we went to school.

"Now use your hankies for your dirty noses," she'd say firmly, "not the cuff of your coat or your jerseys." Children's coat sleeves would be shiny from wiping their runny noses in them.

Granny was not only good with the needle and thread. She could also make nourishing soup with a pot full of bones, free from the butcher, and a handful of barley and lentils. Other times, she'd stew up a rabbit. When it was cooked, she'd call me in.

"Here, Lily," she'd say, handing me the rabbit's head on a saucer, "this will do you good."

I'd sit on the steps outside the main hall door with the saucer on my lap. The children playing around would stop and watch as I scooped out the eyes and the brains.

"It tastes just like marrow out of bones," I'd say, licking my finger.

Granny knew everything that was good for you. During the summer, she would send me down the canal to pick dandelion leaves for her tea. I wouldn't pick the yellow flowers though, because everybody knew that if you did you'd wet the bed that night. I'd arrive home with bunches of limp dandelion leaves in my dirty milk-stained hands. She would take the leaves outside to the tap to wash.

"Come on, Lily," she'd say, "wash your hands, then you can come into my room to look at my cards."

Granny often had friends from her parish visit her. One day a lady brought four dolls to give to me and my three sisters. Granny opened her door and called us in. We stared at the dolls on her table and couldn't believe our eyes.

It wasn't even Christmas!

One of the dolls was different. It had eyes that opened and closed, a rare thing then. Granny's friend stood smiling at us behind the table.

"You can choose a doll each," the lady said kindly.

Granny reached for me.

"You go first, Lily. Take the one that goes to sleep," she suggested quietly.

"I don't want that one, Granny; it's got no shoes," I said, reaching out for the smaller doll with the silver shoes.

Kathleen quickly came forward and took the sleeping doll.

"Ya're Granny's pet," Kathleen grumbled a few days later. "She even gives ya the rabbit's head."

Granny heard her, and the next time she had rabbit stew, she called my sister. "Here you are, Kathleen. I kept the rabbit's head for you this time."

My sister sat down with it and picked at the eyes, then handed it to me.

Granny was in her seventies and received an old-age pension. She gave most of it to Mammy.

"Come with me, Lily, for my few bob," she'd say, putting on her black silk cape.

Mammy would kneel down to button up Granny's best boots. Outside in the street, Granny looked small and frail. She leaned on me as we walked slowly towards the post office on Parnell Square. On the way home, she'd buy a caraway-seed cake.

I suppose that's for her and Mammy tonight, I would think to myself. But I hated caraway-seed cake. Granny would buy me my own special cake on my birthday, a chocolate Swiss roll.

WASN'T SHE A LOVELY CORPSE?

Death was a part of our everyday life and we took it all in our stride. Whenever anyone in a tenement house died, a small white card with a narrow black border would be tacked to the main hall door. The person's name

25

and date of death would be handwritten on the card with the letters "RIP" underneath. While out playing, I would notice neighbours stopping to read a card that had just been tacked to a door.

"TB," I'd hear them murmur as they'd hurry on into Flynn's dairy to get their few messages.

When they were gone, I'd stretch up and try to read the scrawly handwriting so I could run home and tell Mammy who had died. The cards weren't always easy to read, especially when the rain made the ink smudgy, but Mammy always knew who they were.

One day, while I was out walking with Mary, we stopped to read a death card tacked to the door of a small private house down by the canal.

"Let's knock on the door and ask if we can say a prayer for the dead person," Mary suggested.

It didn't seem to matter that we didn't know the people who lived there. Mary was always knocking on tenement room doors asking if she could go in and say a prayer for the dead person. This was my first time.

"Come in," the lady said, pulling the door wide open.

And without hesitation, she pointed to a room upstairs. As we climbed the stairs, her voice floated up from below: "I'd never turn away the prayers of a child."

The door of a bedroom was open. We peeped in. The curtains were drawn, and I immediately recognised the familiar smell of paraffin and Lifebuoy soap. A faint red light glowed from a small altar lamp that stood on a shelf in the corner of the room with a statue of the Blessed Virgin beside it. I was used to seeing this lamp in my pals' homes.

I followed Mary and knelt down with her at the foot of the bed and tried not to look at the still, white face on the pillow or the hands with the rosary beads entwined around them. Instead, my eyes fixed on a large picture of the Sacred Heart hanging over the bed. Mary, with her head bowed and her hands joined, chanted Hail Marys quietly. I didn't know this prayer. I only knew the Our Father, and I didn't think I could say that.

I headed straight for the door when I saw Mary blessing herself and making a move to go. With great relief, I quickly tiptoed down the stairs, out of the house and into the cool, fresh air of the street.

"Wasn't she a lovely corpse?" Mary said with a saintly look on her face.

I nodded in agreement, and deep in thought we walked slowly home.

GRANNY AND UNCLE AL

Every night after Daddy had gone out, Mammy'd tuck us up in bed, turn down the gas globe and slip into Granny's room for a sit down and a chat.

On New Year's Eve, when the boats were blowing their horns on the quays, Granny would become sentimental thinking about her son Al, who was a seaman in the Royal Navy.

"Let's have a glass of port, Dolly, to see the year in," she'd say to Mammy, taking out her small bottle of port that she'd bought for that occasion.

Everyone called Mammy Dolly, a pet name given to her as a child because she was petite, with dark hair and big grey-brown eyes.

Uncle Al never married, and whenever his boat docked in Dublin, he'd be up to see Mammy and Granny straightaway. Mammy's face would beam with delight as he'd grab her up and kiss her.

"Where's Mum, Dolly? Where's Mum?" he'd say.

Mammy'd rush and knock on Granny's door.

"Look who's here, Mum! Look who's here!"

A chair would be cleared for him next to our fire. Granny would sit beside Uncle Al, laughing about his adventures while he drank a big mug of sweet milky tea. Then Mammy would pull me aside and whisper, "Go next door to the dairy; ask Miss Flynn for half a pound of fruit cake; tell her I'll pay her later. Don't be long."

It was great having a visitor. Uncle Al would put his hand in his pocket and shove money into mine to buy sweets. That was great too, except, when he'd be gone, Granny would take the half a crown from me, give it to Mammy and hand me a penny instead.

The last time Uncle Al came to visit, Granny hugged and kissed him goodbye.

"I might not be here when you come again, Al," she joked.

"When you go, Mum, I go," he called back as he closed our door and headed back to the Seamen's Mission.

Granny became ill and stayed in bed Christmas 1938. On New Year's Eve, Mammy was very worried. She ran over to Grafton Street and told Uncle Bob that Granny was dying. Late that night, we were all brought in to see her. My uncle was sitting beside her bed, his head bowed.

"Bob, why is my lamp turned down low?" Granny murmured.

We looked at each other puzzled because the wick was up full, glowing.

"Go over and say goodnight to Granny," Mammy said quietly.

We went up to her bed, one after the other. When it came to Johnny's turn, Granny gave him a ha'penny. This surprised us all, as she was always telling him off, calling him the ruffian. The ha'penny was very old, smooth and shiny, the king's head barely visible. Johnny took one look at it, then threw it back at her.

"That's a bad ha'penny," he said, rushing out of her room.

Mammy was shocked, but Granny laughed, a weak laugh.

We were hurried to bed. My sisters and I tricked around, not ready for sleep. Robbie was sobbing under his bed covers. He looked up and shouted over at us, "Don't youse realise Granny's dying!"

Granny died that night.

"We'll see you tomorrow, Dolly, to make arrangements," Uncle Bob said, leaving.

Mammy ran out of our room, out of the tenement, up Fitzgibbon Street and around and around Mountjoy Square. She knew she'd miss Granny terribly.

Next day, the death card with the narrow black border was tacked to our main hall door. Granny's name was written on it in Mammy's handwriting.

> Ellen Mary Crawte Died 1st January 1939
> The Lord is my Shepherd.

A large black crepe ribbon tied in a bow hung above it. I stood proudly in front of it. At last we had a card on the hall door.

"This is our card and that's my granny's name," I told the other children, not letting them near it.

Two shiny black horses with white plumes pulled the hearse to Mount Jerome Cemetery. These elegant horses were not like the big working horses that pulled the Phoenix Laundry cart or the scraggy looking horse that our ragman led along.

Weeks later, Mammy dragged Granny's trunk into our room, pushed it over to the fire and opened it. It was a cold January day and my sisters and I sat around the fire watching her.

"Do you know," Mammy said with tears in her eyes, "during the Troubles Granny nearly got shot by a Black-and-Tan soldier."

"Why, what happened, Mammy?" Robbie called over from his bed, where he was lying reading a comic.

"It was when we lived on the North Wall. Granny was worried about your Aunt Kitty, who was going out with a British soldier. You see, girls got tarred and feathered on the quays if they went out with a British soldier. Well, one night your Aunt Kitty was very late coming home and Granny was worried. She peeped out a bedroom window watching for her. A soldier standing opposite our house saw Granny. He thought she was a sniper and quickly raised his gun. When Granny turned, he saw the bun at the back of her head and lowered his gun."

Mammy bent down into the trunk, gathered up the last of Granny's private things and threw them into the fire on top of the smouldering ash. Along with the letters went the cards, even the ones with the delicate embroidered lace on front. I watched them shrivel up, then burst into flames.

Uncle Al was buried at sea six months after Granny died.

AUNT LILUM

It was the morning of my baptism and Aunt Lilum, Daddy's big sister, had promised to be my godmother. She met Mammy outside our church in Charles Street.

"I'm sorry, Dolly, but my priest has forbidden me to enter the grounds of a Protestant church," she said, hurrying away.

I was annoyed when Mammy told me this years later.

"Well, why did you call me after her? Why didn't you call me Ellen after Granny?" I complained.

Aunt Lilum had two tall sons, Lenny and Cecil, who, like her, had prominent buck teeth and short curly hair. Her husband was a dentist, but business must have been bad at times because they were for ever having to move. They would sneak out in the middle of the night, pushing a small handcart with all their belongings on it.

Whenever Aunt Lilum came to visit, Mammy would cut a thick slice of bread for us all, including Lenny and Cecil. If she had no jam to spread on the butter, she'd sprinkle sugar. On one of these visits, she sat talking to my aunt at the kitchen table while I walked around eating my bread, happily humming to myself. Lenny followed me, eating his bread with his thick khaki-coloured woollen gloves still on. I tried to keep away from him.

"Why does he keep those horrible gloves on?" I whispered to Mammy when Aunt Lilum went out to the lavatory.

"It's because he has the scabies, the itch between his fingers. He doesn't want anyone to see the sores," Mammy answered quietly.

I accidentally dropped a lump of my bread on the floor. Lenny and Cecil looked at it in horror.

"The good bread, Aunty Dolly! Lily has dropped the good bread," Lenny called out.

Annie and I giggled at him. Looking at Lenny, I dropped some more. Mammy was watching.

"Stop it, Lily," she said crossly.

Mammy was puzzled by Lenny and Cecil's reaction over a crumb being dropped. "They look so well off in those new brown tweed overcoats," she said to us after they were gone. "But God help them, they must have known hunger!"

Something we did not know.

AUNT LILUM WANTS OUR ARMCHAIR

It was a dark day, the sky overcast and full of snow. My sisters and I stood looking out of our window, our noses pressed up against the freezing cold pane, breathing steam, making figures on it with our fingers. We watched as a man coming up our street pushing a handcart laden with two large armchairs stopped outside our window. Letting go of the two long wooden handles of the cart, he straightened up his stooped back and blew hard into his two grubby red hands, rubbing them close together. Then reaching into his overcoat pocket, he pulled out a screwed-up piece of paper. The window in the room above us was pulled up.

"Who are ya looking for?" Mrs Murphy called down.

"O'Sheas," he said gruffly.

"Oh, dey're just below me in de front parlour," she shouted back to him.

"That's us, Mammy!" we cried out.

Mammy, with a puzzled look on her face, hurried over to the window. We all ran to our door and looked out into the hall. The main hall door was wide open and a cold, blustery wind blew in from the street. Mammy held us back as the man struggled in with one of the armchairs on his back.

"I've got anudder one for ya, Missus," he said, as he explained where they'd come from.

While he was bringing in the second chair, we could hear Mrs Murphy's door above us creak. We knew she would be out on the stairs, straining her ears. Dropping the second chair inside our room, he tipped his cap and hurried out to his empty handcart.

Mammy quickly closed our door.

"Daddy's daddy has died," she told us quietly, "and he's left us your granny's armchairs."

The death of Granddad O'Shea meant nothing to me. I had never seen him or Grandma and knew only what Mammy had told us about them

"He was a big man, he was, very demanding," she'd say. "You see, he had once been a garda. Your granny, poor Mrs O'Shea, was like a little old woman, worn out running after him. God help her, she had a big family as well."

Mammy wiped her hands over and over in her apron before she dared to touch the chairs. She rushed around our room: the beds were made, the floor was swept, the table was scrubbed and the fire was stacked up high with cinders. The armchairs were placed on each side of our fire.

I jumped into one of the chairs and curled up in its wide, deep seat, enjoying the feel of it. Putting my face up against one of its massive arms, I tried to get the smell of this thin little granny with the worried face.

Living on the ground floor made it hard for Mammy to keep our room warm. The big, heavy hall door needed a good hard push to close. Mrs Murphy was the only one who did this. Other neighbours left it swinging wide open. The cold north wind would blow through the hall and under our door, so the armchairs were a godsend and made our room cosy. Every night before going to bed, my sisters and I would snuggle up, two in each chair, drinking our hot cocoa and pointing to the pictures we could see in the glowing fire. I had my own special song that I sang as I stared into the fire:

> Blow, blow the fire,
> Make a pretty light.
> In walks a little girl
> All dressed in white,
> White shoes and stockings,
> White curly hair,
> A little muff around her neck,
> And a Sunday hat she wears.

That was my song and I didn't like Annie or Sylvia singing it.

A few weeks later Aunt Lilum came to visit. She became cranky when she saw the armchairs.

"One of those chairs should have been given to me, Dolly Crawte!" she hissed, as frothy spit bubbled out through her bucked teeth.

Even when Aunt Lilum wasn't giving out, her buck teeth stood out so much that it gave her an angry look that frightened me. I kept well away from her.

Mammy sat down and looked worried. Aunt Lilum jumped up to go.

"I don't know why me daddy left the two a' them to ya," she shouted back as she left with her two sons, banging our door behind her.

Aunt Lilum banged our door so hard that our old rusty horseshoe hanging over our door for luck came flying down, giving us all a terrible fright and nearly splitting me open.

That night, when Daddy came in, Mammy told him everything.

"John," she said quietly, "Lilum has been here today, and she was giving out hell about us getting the two chairs. Maybe we should give her one."

Daddy just laughed.

"The cheek of her, the jealous bitch. My father had a soft spot for ya. Don't ya remember him tricking around with ya and embarrassing ya by washing himself in that little tin bath on our landing. 'Hello, Dolly-Daydreams,' he'd call after ya, as ya'd run down the stairs, yer face red as a beetroot."

Mammy laughed.

"Yes, but what I remember, John, is your poor mother running up and down those stairs with pots of hot water trying to keep his bath warm. But what are we going to do about Lilum?"

34

"Nuttin', he's left them to us! She's not getting one a' them. D'ya hear me? They're ours."

Weeks went by and Aunt Lilum continued to knock hard on our door to argue about the chairs. Then one night, I woke up and, crying with fright, told Mammy that I had seen Granny O'Shea in the dark.

"She was pointing to one of her armchairs," I sobbed.

Alarmed, Mammy jumped out of bed.

"Christ almighty, ya're not going to listen to that young wan again are ya?" Daddy shouted as Mammy tried to comfort me.

Only a few weeks before, I had been waking up every night sobbing. "Mammy, there's somebody under yer bed, there's somebody under yer bed," I'd scream, waking everybody up.

Daddy tried to cure me. He jumped up one night and shoved me under his bed.

"It's only a feckin' shadow from the feckin' lamp-post outside," he shouted. "Now go back to sleep, before I murder ya."

I hadn't cried again until now.

Early next morning, I noticed that Mammy was missing and so was one of the armchairs. Hearing a noise outside in the street, I climbed over my sisters, pulled up the curtain and peeped out the window. Aunt Lilum was holding the handle of an old brown pram. Mammy and Robbie were struggling with one of our armchairs awkwardly. They were trying to balance it on top of the pram. Shivering in my vest, I watched Aunt Lilum push this heavy weight, with all her strength, up our street. The wheels of the pram wobbled and squeaked, its hard white tyres skidding around on the slush.

Mammy came back in with Robbie, closing the door quietly behind her. Fixing her apron, she glanced anxiously over to where Daddy lay sleeping, buried down deep in the hollow of their fibre mattress, his overcoat on top of him. She crossed the room and sat down in the remaining armchair.

With a worried look on her face, she glanced at the space where the other armchair had been.

Fumbling around in her apron pocket, she searched for a butt. Her hands trembled as she lit it, and with her eyes half closed, she deeply inhaled and waited – waited for him to wake and the row that was sure to follow.

THE LOST HALF-CROWN

One evening when we were just finishing tea, Mammy put her hand in her apron pocket and was shocked to find that her half-crown was gone.

"Oh my God," she cried out, jumping up from the table. "I didn't know there was a hold in my apron pocket. My half-crown must have slipped out."

"It's nowhere here, Mammy," we said, ducking our heads under the table, our eyes scanning the floorboards for it.

"Oh, it's got to be somewhere in this room," Mammy said hopefully. "I haven't been out all day, and it can't have just vanished."

We searched every corner of the room on our hands and knees, Mammy crawling with us.

"Maybe it fell out when you were making the beds, Mammy," we said, trying to be helpful.

Each bed was quickly stripped apart and blankets and sheets were vigorously shaken, but to no avail.

"Perhaps it rolled under the girls' bed," Johnny's muffled voice came back to us as he crawled on his stomach underneath the sagging spring of our bed.

Wanting to be the one to find it and to please Mammy, I

ran to our one big armchair. My hands plunged down deep on each side of its seat, bringing up fluff, breadcrumbs, buttons, butts of lead pencils and Sylvia's old dummy – the dummy that she had a suck of when she thought no one was looking – but no half-crown.

We soon grew tired of searching and started to fool around with each other, laughing and joking, leaving Mammy to continue the search on her own. She looked at us all crossly.

"That half-crown, I'll have youse all know, was for tomorrow's messages. It's all the money I have in the world!"

Hearing the worried tone in her voice, we reluctantly sauntered around the room, rummaging through the same old spots again. Mammy sat down and went over everything that she'd done that day.

"The fire!" she called out to us, with both relief and alarm. "That's where it is! Sure, of course that's where it is! Didn't I carry the paper and sticks in my apron over to the fire, and it must have fallen in as I leant over to light it."

We often found the remains of things in the ashes the day after they had been accidentally knocked down from the mantelpiece into the fire. So, grabbing the poker, Mammy quickly raked out the hot ashes and scrutinised every little bit of ash, poking it here and there. Slowly and silently, she swept the ashes back under the burning hot bars of the fire.

"It's getting late," she said in a low voice, and, with a heavy sigh, she reached up and turned down the gas globe above the mantelpiece.

As we undressed, we kept glancing over at her anxiously. She was quiet and looked pale. She didn't even tell Johnny off when he started playing around, jumping and squealing on his bed. She just sat down and put her head in her hands.

"God help me. Please God, help me," she murmured.

I felt worried, because the only time I ever heard Mammy praying was when Mr Campbell came on one of his many visits. After sitting with her for a while and listening to her troubles about Daddy not working, he'd hand her a note for Blake's, a Protestant grocer in Meath Street. Then kneeling down, he would lower his head and join his hands.

"Let us say a little prayer now, shall we!" he would say in his posh voice. Mammy would quickly kneel down behind her chair and beckon to me and my sisters to kneel down also.

However, on this night, I watched her sitting there on her own praying.

It's a pity we're not Catholics, I thought to myself. *We could say a prayer to Saint Anthony to help us find it. That's what Missus Murphy always does, and she finds everyt'ing she loses all right.*

Without saying a word, Mammy got up and walked out the door into the dark tenement hall. Lying in bed beside my sisters, I listened to her footsteps as she hurried down the two little steps that led out into the yard. I slipped out of bed and ran after her. She was standing by the washing line – a rope that stretched from one end of the yard to the other – and there on the ground, shining in the moonlight, was the lost half-crown. It had slipped out of her apron pocket when she had reached up to take down her washing.

THE STREET WAS MY PLAYGROUND

"Missus O'Shea, can yer Lily come out to play today?" Mary'd say, after knocking on our door. I played many games with all the other children outside in the street in all weathers. Children would drift into their own age group. Sometimes my pals would have to mind their little brothers or sisters, so we'd take turns keeping an eye on them, running around and shaking pram handles when babies cried.

Skipping was a popular winter game to keep us warm. Someone would be bound to have an old rope. We'd take turns, one holding each end of it while the rest queued up waiting to be called in to skip. We'd sing the name of the person about to jump in:

> There's somebody under the bed.
> Whoever can it be?
> I feel so very nervous
> I call for Lil-ly.
>
> Lily lights the candle.
> Nobody there,
> Hi fi diddly di,
> And out jumps she.

Whenever it was Mary's turn to skip, the boys would run over and chant, "I see Paris, I see France. I see Mary Murphy's pants."

Mrs Murphy would be hanging out her window – as usual.

"Get away from her, youse bloody bowzies," she'd shout down, and the boys would run off laughing.

When we grew tired of skipping, we'd tie our rope to the top of a lamp-post to make a swing. But our skipping ropes would wear out, snap and send us flying out on to the road, landing on our behinds.

It was a godsend when someone would come out dragging a big, thick Guinness rope behind him. His daddy would be after taking it off the Guinness boats where he worked. The ropes were used for holding the barrels together and for lowering them down the cellars of the pubs around Dublin.

Sonny Boy Smith, who lived in the tenement opposite me, would spit on his hands, climb up the iron lamp-post and tie the Guinness rope to the top with a knot. It made a wonderful swing for us all.

We were not supposed to put a rope on the iron lamp-posts because our constant swinging bent them, but the gardaí would turn a blind eye, ignoring us as they sauntered by going back to the barracks that led off Fitzgibbon Street.

When there were no ropes around, Mary would bring out her two tennis balls to play with. Taking turns, we'd bounce the balls, one at a time, up against the side of a tenement wall. With each bounce, we'd sing: "Billy Boland. Biscuit Baker. Ballybough Bridge. Billy Boland. Biscuit Baker. Ballybough Bridge."

Gay Callaghan, a boy who lived next door, would hear us and bring out his whip and top to show off. Gay, an only child, had everything, even a three-wheel bike, which he'd never let anyone touch.

"Let's look at Gay's top," Mary'd say, grabbing up her two balls.

Sitting on the edge of the kerb, Gay would chalk a colourful pattern on his top, then, with all his strength, he'd whip it right across the path. Mary and I would marvel at its spiralling, colourful patterns.

In summer, we girls played piggy-beds on the path outside our tenement window. We needed chalk to make squares and numbers on the path and a piggy-tin to kick from bed to bed. No one had any money to buy chalk, but inside my pals' homes there were lots of statues that were for ever falling and breaking. The broken pieces made excellent chalk. Strangely enough, as if by a miracle, the statues always seemed to fall just at the right time. I'd stand at our railings watching my pals chalking the squares with the broken head of the Child of Prague or a lump of the Sacred Heart. How I used to wish that I were a Catholic and had statues that might fall and break!

Still, I felt very pleased with myself when I found an empty shoe-polish tin in the lane opposite our house, Fitzgibbon Lane. I filled this tin with mud, so as to make it nice and heavy to kick from square to square while I hopped after it.

Every night, I'd hide my piggy-tin in my secret hiding place on top of the cistern in the lavatory out in our back-yard. Standing tiptoe on the lavatory bowl, I'd reach up high to the black iron tank. My hands would fumble among the damp and sticky dust as I pushed my tin in as far as I could, hoping no one would see me, especially that Nit Nah, who lived in our street.

Nit Nah had a harelip. He was a big boy who enjoyed tor-menting girls. Whenever we were playing piggy-beds, he'd kick my piggy-tin and try to pinch it.

"Gimme nah! Gimme nah!" he'd demand.

We'd grab the piggy up, run to our hall door for safety, then shout after him, "Nit Nah! Nit Nah! Nit Nah!"

But it wasn't only Nit Nah who annoyed us girls. There was Deaf-and-Dumb Tommy, who lived in our tenement. He was for ever chasing us, making frightening noises with a wriggly worm between his fingers. When he'd catch us, he'd open his mouth and swallow it.

"Go and play with the boys," we'd scream, hoping he'd hear us.

Boys played games with marbles, rolling them along the gutter. Our Johnny's trousers' pockets were always bulging with marbles he had won from his pals.

Boys were always looking for old bicycle wheels. They'd run for miles with them, whacking them along with their sticks. Once when Daddy was fixing his bike in our room he called Johnny in.

"Ya can take the spare wheel for a hoop," he said, pointing to a rusty old wheel lying on the floor with no tyre.

Johnny, delighted, ran out with his hoop, bowling it along

41

with a little stick. Other boys looked after him enviously as his hoop clattered down our street. One day, he left his hoop outside McClean's sweetshop. He had a ha'penny to spend on bull's-eyes. When he came out his hoop was gone.

"Even me stick was robbed," he sobbed later to Mammy.

"Maybe Hairy Lemon took it," Sylvia suggested.

"Hairy Lemon wouldn't take it," Mammy said smiling.

We all burst out laughing at the thought of Hairy Lemon, with his yellow prickly face, bowling Johnny's hoop up our street.

Hairy Lemon spent his days shuffling along the gutters looking for cigarette butts.

"Giss yer butt, Mister! Giss yer butt!" we'd hear him beg from men passing by.

He didn't chase us when we called after him, not like Irish Annie. Irish Annie was a thin, hunched-up, elderly woman with long black hair and a pointy nose. She also lived on the streets. She'd come up our street, stop outside our house and lean on the railings in front of our window. After a while, she'd crouch down on the steps. One by one, we'd gather in front of her. She'd look up from her old dark shawl and swear at us in Irish. We'd laugh and chant, "Irish Annie! Irish Annie! Irish Annie! Irish Annie!"

But we'd run like mad, screaming, when she'd jump up and swing her small bundle at us. Mothers hanging out of their windows would hear us.

"Get off wid youse and play. An' leave dat poor woman alone!" they'd shout down.

The tenement women were kind to Irish Annie and often filled her tin with sweet milky tea. She'd come and go, sleeping in tenement halls, getting food wherever she could. One morning she was found dead behind a tenement hall door. The night before, she had been seen buying a half pound of Lifebuoy soap.

"She went behind an open tenement hall door and washed herself," I heard Mrs Murphy tell Mammy next morning.

"God help her," Mrs Murphy said sadly, "she must a'known she was goin' t'die, Dolly. Dat's why she washed herself. Sure dat's why de Banshee's being cryin' every night."

We all knew about the Banshee, and we knew that if we heard her cat-like cry outside a house three nights in a row, someone in that house would die.

I had a very clear picture of the Banshee in my mind. I imagined her to be a witch-like character with long black straight hair that swept down to the ground. Everybody said that she combed her hair all the while she whined. Whenever we saw a comb with broken teeth on the ground, we'd all stand and stare in awe of it.

We'd pull each other back: "Come away from it! It's the Banshees' comb. Ya'll have terrible bad luck if ya dare to touch it."

One day, I heard two women talking about the Banshee.

"C'mere till I tell ya," said one to the other. "Did ya hear de Banshee last night crying outside number 35? Dat's the t'ird night in a row. I hear awl Murphy's sick again. He must be going soon!"

I ran in and told Mammy.

"Don't mind them," she said. "Mister Murphy's not going anywhere. If he's going anywhere, it'd be down to the pub. It might be poor Luke at the top of the house though. He's very sick. And don't you remember what Granny used to say: the Banshees are only wild cats."

But I knew there were Banshees and I knew there were ghosts. We told ghost stories around the lamp-posts every night, and during the winter we played my favourite game, the ghost in the hall.

One of us would volunteer to be the ghost. There were eight flights of stairs, and every second flight had a landing and a couple of rooms where a family lived. In the cold winter's evening, it would be creepy hiding on your own, crouching in the quiet, dark corners of our tenement hall. We'd get such a fright if we bumped into a man's bike or a baby's pram resting on the landing. However, we'd feel comforted by the familiar sound of a baby crying and the homely smell of coddle drifting from under the doors. After a few minutes, when the ghost was sure that we were all hidden, she would slowly climb up each stair. The ghost called us all Mary:

> Mary, I'm on the first step.
> Mary, I'm on the second step.
> Mary, I'm on the third step.

When she reached the first landing, her voice would drop to a whisper: "Mary, I'm on the first landing."

We'd all tremble in fear.

When the ghost felt your presence, she would grab you and shout, "Mary, I have ya!"

We'd let out a loud scream in fright. Our screams brought all the doors open. And after repeatedly warning and telling us to be quiet, a mother would lose her temper.

"Will youse all, for God's sake, play outside in the street. Youse are after waken up t'baby! I swear t'God, I'll murder youse!"

WALKING IN AVE

I wanted to be the same as the other children: have statues and altar lamps and a holy water font that I could dip my fingers in and bless myself as I ran in and out of our room. Even playing outside in the street, they could do lots of things that I couldn't do.

Whenever a priest passed by, my pals would leave the game and run up to him.

"God bless you, Father!" they'd say. He would put his hand on their heads.

"God bless you, my child," he'd answer, without stopping.

When a nun would pass by, they'd run up to her: "God bless you, Sister!"

"God bless you, my child," she'd answer, hurrying on.

Priests and nuns were for ever passing up and down our street. As a child, it didn't seem fair to me that my pals were getting all these blessings and I was getting none. I felt left out. It seemed like I was not part of a game they were all playing.

One year, my pals began to prepare for their first holy communion. I pestered my mother.

"Mammy, why can't I make my communion like everyone else is, even Mary is?"

"Because we are not Catholics, that's why! We don't make our communion like the Catholics do. When you are older, you will be confirmed," she would answer in exasperation.

Mary boasted about her new clothes.

"My mammy bought me a lovely new white communion dress that goes right down to the ground an' a new blue coat. An' next week, Lily O'Shea, I'm having me photo taken in Ross Studios wearin' all me new communion clothes."

After the children had been to chapel and received their first communion, mothers would go around showing them off to relatives and neighbours. The first to knock on our door was Mrs Murphy.

Mary stood beaming in front of me.

"Open yer coat, Mary, and show Missus O'Shea yer dress."

Mary opened her coat and lifted her dress a little, revealing her dainty white ankle-strap shoes.

"God love her, she looks lovely," Mammy said, fumbling in her apron pocket for her purse.

Mary looked different all dressed up with her long white veil draped over her ringlets. Her mammy had curled her hair with rags the night before.

I wish I had a veil like that, I thought to myself.

A soft white handbag covered in tiny beads was clutched tightly in her white-gloved hands.

She opened her bag.

"Look, Missus O'Shea, how much money I've collected!" Mary said, holding it up.

Mammy dropped a penny in. And I thought that was unfair too. *I'll never get communion money.*

All the children in our tenement house making their first holy communion knocked on our door. Mammy never turned any away without giving them something. She knew it was a great hardship for the mothers, trying to dress their children on this special day. Mothers who had nothing to pawn would have had to borrow from moneylenders, and there were a few of them around. So the money the children collected often went back to the moneylenders. The pawn-shops would be busy for weeks after.

Another blow was to hit me that summer – the street processions.

One Sunday afternoon, children appeared on the streets wearing their first holy communion clothes again, veils and all.

"What are youse doin' now?" I asked them.

"We're Walking in Ave," they said.

Even the big girls, who had made their communion years before, were walking in the procession. It didn't matter that their dresses were old, creased and halfway up their backs and their veils off-white. They were going to Walk in Ave with everyone else.

Standing at our tenement hall door, I watched them

passing on their way to the procession, their hair combed and faces scrubbed.

I hurried after them. Mary looked back at me.

"Me mammy said ya can't Walk in Ave, Lily O'Shea, 'cause ya're not a Catholic!"

Pretending not to care, I turned away and tried to whistle.

"An' ya should not be whistling either, Lily O'Shea, 'cause every time a girl whistles, Our Lady cries."

Crowds of children congregated outside a chapel near Gardiner Street. I stood on the path envying them. Hands joined, as if to pray, they walked behind the priests singing, "Ave, Ave, Ave Maria. Ave, Ave, Ave Maria."

I followed on the path behind them. For days after my sisters and I would play at Walking in Ave. With a bit of old lace curtain on our heads, we walked around our room singing, "Ave, Ave, Ave, Maria."

MOUNTJOY SQUARE

The street was my playground and Mountjoy Square was my park; that was, when I could get into it.

Mountjoy Square was at the top of my street. This four-acre square of tall trees, bushes and narrow gravel paths was surrounded by high spiked iron railings. The square was named after Lord Mountjoy, who had owned a lot of property around it in the last century. It had been established for the sole use of the gentry who had once lived in the tall red-bricked Georgian houses. Each of these residents had been given a key to the gates to enjoy the park at their leisure.

Though the Corporation had acquired the park in the late thirties, they wanted to keep it as one of the nicest parks in the city, so a key-holder kept the large gates firmly locked, guarding its four corners from the swarms of children that played on the paths outside. But the park was a temptation to us children, and the locked gates could not stop us from trying to break in.

Boys playing football on the road would often kick their ball over the railings into the park accidentally. After a lot of shouting and swearing, one of the lads would grip hold of the bars.

"I'll climb over. Just gimme a leg up."

Although I never saw a boy being impaled on these spiked railings, I had heard terrible stories from other children of its happening.

"Oh God, Lily," Mary would say, blessing herself, "me mammy told me a young fella was stuck on top of the spikes yesterday and blood was all comin' out a' him. God, isn't that awful?"

Children tried to squeeze through the railings, especially small boys, and the one with the big head always got stuck. In his fright to free himself, he would try to pull his head out; but the more he pulled, the more his head would get stuck, hurting his ears. His face would go red as he screamed, louder and louder, "Mammy! Mammy! Mammy!"

The terrified screams of the child would bring all the mothers rushing over from the tenement doorways.

"Jesus, it's me young fella," a mother would cry, grabbing hold of him and trying to pull his head out.

"Wait, Missus, I'll get a bit a' butter," one of the other women would shout, running back across the road to her tenement room.

Crowding around, we'd all watch with interest while the boy's mother frantically rubbed the butter up and down on the bars and around his ears trying to release him. Men

48

passing by would stop and try their best to bend the bar back. Secretly we hoped they couldn't, so that the fire engine would have to be sent for. The firemen in their big red helmets would soon saw through the bar and prise it back.

"Now, aren't you the bold boy," one of the firemen would laugh, lifting the boy out.

"God bless ya," the boy's mother'd say, holding the child into her.

Then, spitting on a corner of her apron, she'd wipe his dirty nose and scrub his tear-stained face. We'd wave to the firemen as they drove away, leaving the broken bar pushed to one side. One after the other, we'd squeeze through the broken bar into Mountjoy Square and play hide-and-seek and chasey among its lovely trees and bushes. But not for long. Soon the railings would be repaired again and we'd be back on the paths playing piggy-beds.

Each evening when we'd grow tired of playing, we'd sit on the edge of the kerb, watching the big girls coming home from work with their boyfriends.

"When I grow up," I'd say to my pals, "I'm going to have me hair up on top just like they have."

As our tenement hall had no light, courting couples looking for privacy would linger behind the hall door. While lying in bed at night with my face up against the wall, I'd hear them laughing and whispering. And when Mammy's back was turned, I'd climb out of bed, open our door quietly and peep out into the hall. Their cigarettes would be glowing red in the dark and I'd smell the chips they were eating. In the morning they would be gone, leaving behind their greasy newspaper with a few hard chips inside.

I wish I had a boyfriend, then I could have some chips, I'd think to myself, kicking the paper.

One day, I discovered a loose bar in Mountjoy Square's railings. I slipped in and spoke to a man sitting on a seat.

From then on, every morning, instead of playing in the street with the other children, I'd make my way up to the square.

"Mammy, I'm goin' to meet me boyfriend," I'd call out, before closing the door. My mother would nod and think no more of it.

I'd run through the hall and jump down the wide stone steps to the path outside. Children would be in the street, busily tying a rope to the lamp-post outside our window. Up Fitzgibbon Street I'd run, across the road to the square and slip through the loose bar into the park. I'd skip along the gravel path in between the trees until I came to a green wooden seat where I knew he would be sitting. Hearing me coming, he'd look up from his paper and smile. He had a kind face and was smartly dressed, and I thought he was my very own friend. Sitting on the edge of the seat, I'd take my sandals off and bang the gravel out. He'd continue to read.

"Me daddy knocked over the dresser again and all the cups and saucers got smashed," I'd say, looking at him quizzically.

Folding his paper slowly, he'd look at me.

"When do you go back to school?"

"When I go back to school, I will be nine," I'd answer, tucking my dress under me.

I'd stay for a little while talking about my teacher, then I'd hurry off.

"I'll see you again tomorrow," I'd call back to him.

He'd nod and smile.

Weeks passed, and Annie became curious and followed me. That evening at tea, she blurted it out.

"Mammy, I saw Lily talking to a man in Mountjoy Square. She goes to see him every day. That's who she calls her boyfriend," she said, proud of herself for having discovered my secret.

Mammy stopped cutting up the loaf of bread and stared at me.

"Have you been going up there on your own, Lily?"

"That's no harm," I said, grabbing a piece of bread and butter.

Mammy said no more till late that night when she was washing my face and scrubbing my legs.

"Lily," she said firmly, "don't ever go near that man again. D'ya hear me? Play outside in the street where I can see you and, for God's sake, keep away from that Mountjoy Square."

FLEAS, HOPPERS AND BREADCRUMBS

"That child's head's lousy," Daddy'd say when he'd see me continuously scratching my head. Then snatching his coat off the bed, he'd shake it and hurry on out.

"T'God only knows where," Mammy always said.

But we knew he was gone down to the quays to play cards.

"C'mere t'me," Mammy'd say, grabbing hold of me and pulling my head down on her lap.

Finding my hair full of nits, she'd jump up and reach for the dreaded fine comb. She kept this comb handy behind one of the collie dogs on our high mantelpiece. Everything important got shoved behind those big dogs: the rent book, the scissors, the reel of black thread and the large darning needle. The dogs stood guarding them.

Mammy would spread a newspaper over one end of the table.

"Lily, will you hold your head well over, for God's sake," she'd snap as she scraped the comb through my scalp.

I was impatient and hated my hair hanging over my face, but when the little grey fleas began to plop down on to the paper, I'd stay still, counting them. I'd think about the girl who sat in front of me at school. When the sun caught her hair, the little grey fleas surfaced and circled in and out of her ringlets.

"Can I go now?" I'd whinge. "There's no more. Me neck's hurtin'."

Letting go of my head, Mammy would examine the comb, making sure there were no fleas stuck between its fine teeth. Then gathering up the newspaper, she'd hold each end up carefully so as not to drop any. Before I ran off, I'd watch her shake the paper over the fire and I'd listen for the cracks as the fleas dropped on to the red-hot cinders.

Running through the hall towards the street, my head still tingling, my face red and sweaty, I could hear Mammy's voice trailing after me as she combed Annie's hair.

"I'm fed up with your hairs licking up fleas from others. I swear t'God, I'll get Austin to bring his sharp scissors next time and get him to cut your hairs up short."

Austin was an old friend of Mammy's. She had known him since she was single, and every so often he'd drop in to see her. I was usually playing outside when I'd spot him in the distance cycling slowly up our street. Leaving the other children, I'd run like mad into our room to tell Mammy.

"Mammy, Austin's comin'! Austin's comin'!"

"Oh my God; quick, help me tidy up, Lily," she'd say, kicking our dirty clothes under the bed. Then she'd quickly fix her long black hair up and straighten her apron.

Leaning his bike against the wall in our hall, Austin would knock gently on our door.

"Mammy, it's Austin," I'd smile, opening the door and acting surprised.

I'd stay in when Austin came. We didn't have many visitors, only our clergyman, Mr Campbell. Mammy would shove the kettle on the fire to make Austin a cup of tea. Sitting on the end of my bed, I'd stare at his black curly hair.

Austin would make himself at home. Bending down, he'd pull his bicycle clips off and put them in his pocket. He'd have his good socks on, no holes in the heels like Daddy's, and he'd look very clean with his snow-white shirt under his navy suit jacket.

Mammy would tell him all the news about us children, the things we said and got up to. Austin would burst into his loud, hearty laugh, the heartiest laugh I ever heard. Mammy's face would flush as she laughed with him. Austin had no children and loved hearing about us. And sometimes he'd talk about Daddy.

"You know, Dolly," I heard him say once, "John's the best swimmer on the quays. He goes right under those big cargo boats and comes up the other side."

"I know," Mammy said proudly, "I know. Only the other week, he dived into the quays and saved a man from drowning. The man is well off and is going to buy him a new suit."

I'd let on not to listen and lean up against the end of our bed, fiddling with the brass knob, pulling it off, blowing into it and putting it back on again. But the smile would soon leave my face when I'd see Austin stub his cigarette out in a saucer and take out his large silver scissors.

"You first, Lily," he'd laugh, his blue eyes sparkling. "Kneel up on the back of that chair."

Mammy would take off her apron and tie it around my shoulders. As Austin straightened my head, I could get the smell of tobacco from his brown-stained fingers.

"Close your eyes and keep your head still," he'd say, becoming serious. He'd cut my brown hair short and even.

"She'll have no fleas now," he'd laugh, shaking the hairs from Mammy's apron into the fire.

Down I'd jump and run out into the street to find Annie.

"Ya're wanted now, Annie. Austin's in there waiting for ya!"

Fleas were not the only problem. Hoppers plagued our beds.

"I'll have to look in your bed today for hoppers," Mammy would sigh when she saw red welts on our arms and legs.

She'd spend hours and hours examining all three beds for fleas and hoppers. Coming in from playing in the street, I'd find her sitting on the edge of our bed, scrutinising our blankets. I'd sit beside her and help search for the brown hoppers. I'd watch how she squashed them between her thumbnails.

"Is that our blood?" I'd say, shocked at the sight of the red bloodstains on her nails.

The grey fleas were easier to detect and kill, especially in our coarse red blanket, a blanket like the ones in Jervis Street Hospital.

"Where do they come from?" I'd ask Mammy as I dragged the blanket over my lap and searched.

"The turf is full of hoppers; you can't get rid of them."

I'd look around at the turf stacked next to the fireplace.

The edges of the blankets were loosely sewn over with big stitches. I'd pull them open till I found a flea or a hopper.

"Look," I'd shout, excited, "there's millions of them in here."

Mammy would quickly nudge me and point towards the door.

"Keep your voice down," she'd whisper. "Someone might be passing through the hall and hear you."

Everyone in the tenements had the same trouble with fleas and hoppers, but they kept their business to themselves in case neighbours thought they were dirty. Some even had bugs.

"Thank God, we haven't got bedbugs," Mammy would say, relieved, straightening the blankets over our bed. "They come out at night, pierce your skin and suck the blood out of you."

We'd all look at her horrified. Fleas and hoppers seemed quite friendly when we'd hear about bugs!

Bugs were reddish-brown insects with little legs. They bred in the walls of tenements behind old loose wallpaper and inside the mattresses and bed springs. Mammy would know as soon as she entered a tenement room whether there were bugs or not.

"Oh, you can easily tell," she'd say. "The room has a distinct, bad, musty smell."

When Mammy wasn't looking, we'd play on the beds, jumping around. Bang! The spring base would slip off a corner of the bed ends and crash to one side.

"Get off the bed, all of youse, for God's sake, before I murder youse," Mammy would shout, struggling to lift the heavy spring base back up on to the iron bed ends again.

The mattresses were filled with loose fibre. Every few months, they'd become lumpy. Mammy would rip up one end of the mattress cover and empty the fibre on to the floor. If she could afford it, she'd replace it, but most of the time she'd have to tease the fibre out and stuff it back again, leaving small piles of red dust on the floor. She'd have no trouble getting us to bed that night. I loved lying on the clean and restuffed mattress. Although it would be prickly, it was like floating on a high mountain. But the mattress would soon flatten down and be lumpy again.

Our bed was up against the wall. Most of the time, my sisters and I slept at the top, our heads on a long bolster pillow. We fought to get next to the wall, where no one could pull the clothes off you and you had less chance of being pushed out during the night. For a change, we'd sleep two at the top and two at the bottom, and every so often we'd sleep sideways.

The steel spring base that our mattress rested on had a big hole in the centre. Sometimes the mattress would sink down the hole, and my sisters and I would slide down with it to the floor. Mammy would frequently mend the hole with twine, like a darn.

Having got us all settled in bed, Mammy would lower the gas globe. The fire would be dropping. Bending down, she'd stick a small piece of twisted paper through the bars of the fire, then blowing it hard, she'd light her cigarette butt. She would have saved this butt in her apron pocket for this moment. After a few puffs, the butt would be thrown into the fire. Coming over to our bed, she'd lean over to tuck us in. Often, I'd still be awake.

"Mammy, can I have a bit a' bread, I'm starvin', an' can ya sprinkle sugar on it?"

While I'd be sitting munching it, my sisters would wake up and want some too. Finished eating, we'd all lie down again, but not for long.

"Mammy, we can't get t'sleep. There's crumbs in the bed."

"Right, out of the bed, all of youse, till I brush the sheet. Youse have me heart scalded."

Out we'd all come, one by one, and stand shivering in our vests. Back in bed, she'd throw the sheet and blanket over us. She'd be giving out hell as she tucked us in, this time really tightly.

"Now hurry up and go to sleep or youse'll never wake up in the mornin'!"

Outside in the street, it would be quiet. The only sounds would be the occasional singing of a drunk passing by our window, or the banging of our heavy hall door as neighbours passed through on their way upstairs to their rooms.

OUR RAGMAN

Dan the Ragman came up Fitzgibbon Street every few months. He was a stern-looking man dressed in a shabby grey dustcoat and cap. Sometimes he'd be pushing a handcart loaded with rags; other times he'd be leading his scraggy old horse that was pulling his cart.

"Rags, bottles and bones. Rags, bottles and bones," he'd shout.

Buried beneath the piles of rags on his cart were boxes of cheap plain-white delph which he'd exchange for rags and jam jars. Colourful cellophane windmills on sticks were displayed all around his cart. These windmills seemed magical to us children, as they changed into the most wonderful bright-coloured patterns when the breeze spun them round and round.

Children, hearing his voice, would appear from nowhere. They'd crowd around him and beg him for a windmill or a sweet from one of his jars. Dan was a shy man with the women and would do all his bargaining through the children.

"Go an' ask yer mammy if she has any rags or empty jam jars," he'd say, shaking his jar of sweets.

Windows would be lifted, one after the other, and mothers would call out, "Send a child up, Dan, while I get a bundle ready."

The mothers would be desperate for delph. Their husbands were for ever coming home drunk, and, at the least sign of an argument, they'd pick up their dinner and throw it into the fire – plate and all.

In the hope that I might get a windmill or a sweet, I'd run home, burst open the door and shout, "Mammy, have ya got any rags for Dan?"

"Jesus, is he out there already? I didn't hear him. I need some delph."

Mammy'd search around and make me up a bundle.

"Try and get me a cup, saucer and plate," she'd say, holding my arm.

After I ran back with a bundle to Dan, he would examine it and frown.

"Go back and tell yer mammy that I need more rags for the plate."

Mammy, wanting this plate, would frantically search through our clothes. She would drag out old cardigans and frocks and hold them up to us to see what we'd outgrown.

While she pulled the buttons off, I'd watch the cart slowly pass our window. I'd be worried sick he might go, my hopes of a windmill fading.

"Hurry, Mammy! Hurry, he's goin'," I'd whine, anxiously jumping up and down.

My pals were doing the same thing, running backwards and forwards to Dan. While all this bargaining was going on, Mrs Murphy would be watching curiously from her open window to see who was getting what. Resting on her folded arms, she would lean out and have a bit of a laugh with Dan.

"Don't send de childer up, Dan. Come up yerself and get me! Sure dat's all I am – a bundle of rags and bones!"

This would cause an uproar of laughter from all the other women leaning out of their windows. They'd forget their worries for a little while as laughter echoed through the tenements.

THE BIG MATCH

"Mammy," I shouted as I dashed out the door, "can I go down to Croke Park with Mary? The big match is on today."

Croke Park football ground was close to Fitzgibbon Street. Although there were lots of matches played here during the year, the big match, the All-Ireland (football) Final, was the one we looked forward to the most. It wasn't that we were interested in the match itself; few of us girls understood the game, and Mammy and Daddy certainly didn't talk about it.

We'd arrive at Croke Park hours before the match was due to begin. Close to the gates, men would be busily setting up large wooden boards. We knew not to get in the way of these pale, thin-faced men in their greasy caps. They'd glare at us as they covered their boards in rosette badges and bright-coloured hats displaying the teams' names. But the boards that interested us were the ones lined with flesh-coloured gelatine dolls dressed in the teams' colours. These dolls, with their bright happy faces, were four inches long with lots of soft feathers billowing out from their waists. It didn't matter to us that their long legs were joined together. We wanted one and would have hours of fun sitting on the tenement steps making clothes for them out of small bits of rags. If I got one, I'd put the doll in an empty sweet box that Flynn's had given me, tie a piece of string to one end and drag it along, letting on it was a pram.

We'd watch the men arriving for the match. Most were from the country. They'd have come up by train and booked into a boarding house for the weekend. Chatting away, they'd buy a doll or badge and pin it to the lapels of their best tweed jackets.

Back home we'd dawdle and wait patiently outside our

house for the match to be over, all the while listening to the roars and cheers as the goals were scored. At last the match would finish; when the loud cheers had stopped, the dead silence told us so.

Fitzgibbon Street, the shortest way back to the city, was the most likely route the men would take when the game was over. We'd stand up on the highest step outside our tenements and watch eagerly as the crowds of men started to make their way up our street, laughing and talking loudly. These giants of well-dressed countrymen, with their fresh, ruddy complexions, would walk on the roads as well as the paths. The Dublin men looked quite small in comparison.

Mothers leaning out of tenement windows would watch the crowds of men coming closer and closer.

Mrs Murphy would shout down to us, "In de name a' God, will one of youse get dat child in before she's trampled on!"

Other mothers would come down from their rooms and stand quietly behind us. They'd lean against their hall doors holding their babies and stare at the crowd.

We'd wait till a countryman who was proudly displaying his doll on his lapel came near our tenement. There wouldn't be much hope of getting one of these dolls from a Dublin man. He'd more than likely have had just the price of his ticket and, if he did have a doll, he'd be sure to have a child at home waiting for it. The countryman would be our only chance.

"Did ya win the match, Mister?" we'd shout, hoping they had.

"Shure, begad we did," they'd laugh back in their broad Cork or Kerry accents.

"Can we have yer doll, please? G'wan, give us it!" we'd shout putting our hands out.

All the while walking, their long legs taking huge strides towards the city, they'd unpin their dolls and pass them over to us.

The countrymen, having come up to Dublin for the big match, would make the most of their weekend. They'd enjoy themselves in the many pubs and dance halls around Dublin that night.

On the Crossbar of My Father's Bike

"C'mon, Lily, I'll take ya to Dollymount. We'll get a few cockles," Daddy said one summer evening when Mammy told him she had nothing for tea.

How surprised and delighted I was! Not only was I going to the seaside, but he had chosen me above my sisters to sit on the crossbar of his bike.

It seemed like no time at all before Daddy was cycling along the busy Clontarf Road that led to Dollymount. Sitting on the crossbar of his bike, I watched the buses passing packed with tired-looking people on their way home from work. I was enjoying every minute and took in everything I saw.

"Look at those lovely hall doors, Daddy!" I shouted as we rode by grand private houses.

The doors were covered with colourful striped canvases to protect them from the sun and sea air. They had special openings for their brass letter boxes and knockers.

"D'ya smell the sea?" Daddy said, pointing to a low stone wall on the opposite side to us.

Crossing over this busy road, he cycled up on to a long wooden platform that led into Dollymount Strand and the sea. Young couples were sauntering along the edge of this platform, their arms linked together. A strong sea breeze blew towards us. My lips tasted salty. As we bumped along on the platform, I leaned back close against Daddy and felt happy and safe. The tide was out, so he cycled down on to the damp sand out as far as he could. Then dropping his bike, he bent down and showed me the signs to look for.

"See those tiny suckin' pinholes, Lily? That's where they are," he said, digging down deep with his hands.

I jumped up and down with delight each time I dug and found one. Soon I grew tired of that game. Tucking my dress inside my knickers, I ran into the freezing sea that lapped gently close by, unaware of the dangerous "swally holes" that Dollymount was known for.

Mammy had given us a large bucket to carry the cockles home in. When Daddy felt he'd collected enough, he called me back, and with the bucket hanging out of the handlebars, we headed for home. The bottom of my dress and knickers were soaking wet from the sea. But that didn't bother me. I had enjoyed myself.

Mammy quickly emptied the cockles into our enamel basin to wash the sand off them.

"Let's feel the cockles," I said to Annie. We put our hands into the basin, playing with them, trying to open their hard ridged shells.

"I can smell the sea off them," she said, leaning over the basin sniffing.

Mammy had a pot of water boiling on the fire ready for the cockles to be cooked in. When she removed these small grey shells from the pot, they opened easily. Inside were creamy-coloured cockles tinged with orange. They had a delicious salty taste from the sea.

After my trip to Dollymount, Daddy would often take me out on his crossbar. One day he decided he would take me to visit one of his friends who lived in a room on the south side of the city. Skilfully, he cycled in between the buses in

O'Connell Street. I clung on tightly to the handlebars as he dodged around horses and carts carrying heavy loads. Messenger boys on bikes were puffing and panting along, their huge baskets in front of their bikes crammed full of groceries they had yet to deliver.

"Jaysus, look at that other poor young fella over there pushing that heavy handcart full of awl sewing machines," Daddy laughed, pointing to a boy who was holding up the traffic.

The buses were beeping and the cars were hooting. In all this confusion, I didn't notice that one of my sandals had slipped off. Although this sandal was well worn and ripped at the back, it was all I had to wear.

"Me sandal, Daddy! Me sandal! It's gone!"

My father stopped as soon as he could at the edge of the road, and I stayed sitting on the crossbar while he rested his foot on the kerb.

"Go back and find me sandal, Daddy," I begged him.

He looked back at the traffic.

"Jesus Christ, Lily, have a heart! Ya don't expect me to go back in all that feckin' traffic to look for yer sandal, now do ya? The buses an' the horses an' carts will have gone all over it by now."

I thought of the times when I had called for Betty, who lived in a freezing cold stable in the Barrack Lane. She wouldn't be let out because she had no shoes to wear. I was terrified that this might happen to me. It was all right for the boys to go barefoot in the street, but neighbours would talk if a girl did.

"I won't be able to go out any more!" I cried.

Men walking by heard me sobbing. They turned around and glared back icily at my father.

"It's the feckin' last time I'll take ya out. Ya're makin' a bleedin' show a' me," he muttered between his teeth.

Sighing, he dug his hands down deep into his pocket and counted out every penny and ha'penny he had. Then taking his foot off the kerb, he slowly peddled along saying nothing to me. Suddenly, he stopped outside a children's shoe shop.

"C'mon in, an' I'll see if I can buy ya a new pair," he said, propping his bike up against the shop window.

I could not believe my ears, and before he could change his mind, I quickly wiped my tear-stained face with the bottom of my dress, and with my one sandal still on, I limped in shyly behind him.

Bundles of children's brown leather sandals hung over the doorway of this shop. There was that special smell of new leather that only shoe shops have. Each wall had shelves that reached right up to the ceiling, stacked high with rows and rows of white shoe boxes. I watched hopefully as the assistant ran up and down a ladder looking for a pair of sandals my size and also at a price Daddy could afford. I was overjoyed when he finally found me a pair. I couldn't wait to get straight home to tell Mammy the whole story and show off my brand new brown sandals to my sisters. And that was the last time he took me out on his crossbar.

I'm Only Lettin' On

"What's that over there, Lily?" Daddy would say, holding his teaspoon in his boiling hot cup of black tea.

I'd look around and he'd quickly place the hot spoon on the back of my hand. Seeing me jump, he'd roar with laughter, nudging me to laugh with him. But I soon learned how far I could go in playing a joke on him.

It was early one morning and I had been sent out to play. Feeling high spirited, I ran back through the hall, opened up the door of our room and shouted, "Mammy! Mammy! Mr Campbell's coming. You better get Daddy up. Quick! Quick!"

Mr Campbell came every week with suggestions as to where Daddy might find work. Mammy was bent over a basin of dirty washing on the table.

"Oh my God," she said, quickly drying her hands on the bottom of her apron. Mr Campbell always shook hands.

Daddy was asleep, sunk down deep in the hollow of the mattress, his head hidden under the covers. Mammy leaned over the bed and shook him.

"Jesus, John! Get up! Get up! Mr Campbell's coming up the street. The room's in a mess and the slop bucket's not even emptied."

Although we were poor, Mammy had her pride and respect for the clergy. She rushed around the room: blankets were dragged up over unmade beds, dirty washing was kicked underneath and the sudsy basin was slid into a corner next to the scrubbing brush and floor cloth. An old rag was thrown over the slop bucket. Daddy fell around the place as he pulled his trousers on.

"Where's me shaggin' shoes and socks?" he hissed, fumbling under his bed.

He felt his chin and ran his fingers through his hair. Mammy straightened her apron and brushed down a chair ready for Mr Campbell. I looked at my father. He looked back at me.

"I'm only lettin' on!" I grinned.

He went white with temper. Chairs were knocked over as he made to grab me.

"If I get hold a' her, I'll fuckin' murder her!"

I ran from the door as fast as I could, across the street and down Fitzgibbon Lane.

I hid there for hours, watching our hall door, hoping he'd go out.

Fed up waiting, I crossed the street and pressed up against the railings outside our window to peer in. Annie was looking out at me, her head in front of our curtain. She had a grin on her face that said, *I can be in, Lily; you have to stay out.*

BIDDY SMYLY'S PRODDY HOME

Mammy was going into Mercer Street Hospital to have an operation. She hadn't been well since Sylvia was born.

Mr Campbell made temporary arrangements for us four girls to be taken into the Birds' Nest, a Protestant home in Dún Laoghaire – known to the Catholic mothers as "Biddy Smyly's Proddy Home". Brigid Smyly, a religious, caring woman, had been the founder of this home in the last century.

"This is a good home, Mrs O'Shea; they'll be well looked after," Mr Campbell reassured Mammy.

Daddy was to mind the boys.

Mr Campbell came with his wife in their car to bring us to the home. It was unusual to see a motor car stop outside a tenement. It could only mean the family were in some sort of trouble. Windows were lifted, and Mrs Murphy and other neighbours leaned out and stared down at us curiously.

"God love them. They're off t'Biddy Smyly's," they called over to each other.

Women standing around our main hall door moved aside to let us pass. Mr Campbell, dressed in a dark suit and white collar, smiled kindly as he opened the back door of his car and ushered us in. It was the first time I had ever been in a car. Before climbing in, we looked back at our pals enviously. They were all out playing piggy-beds and swinging on the lamp-post. Mr Campbell drove through the city, past tenements where crowds of children were playing outside. His wife turned around towards us smiling. She was a small, plump lady and looked posh in her smart suit and hat. We did not know her. We only ever saw her at the yearly seaside excursions to Killiney.

"Have a sweet, dear," she said, holding out a small paper bag full of large luscious sweets – sweets like we had never tasted before.

Whenever we had sweets, they were honey bees: small brown toffees wrapped in paper with pictures of little bees. Maclean's sold them for ten a penny. We sucked Mrs Campbell's expensive sweets silently. As she leaned over towards us with another sweet, a lovely scent drifted from her silk blouse. I liked it, but I missed the homely smell of Lifebuoy soap from Mammy's clean apron.

Where are we going? I wondered, watching lamp-post after lamp-post disappear.

Although the Birds' Nest was only ten miles drive outside Dublin, to us city children it was like another country we were being taken to. We huddled together, staring out at the quiet streets in Dún Laoghaire, puzzled as to why there were no children playing outside. Mr Campbell slowed up and steered the car through two high iron gates that led to the side entrance of the home. The immense size of this building overwhelmed us. He climbed out of the car and opened our door. We trailed across a yard after him. His wife stayed behind. We had nothing to carry, nothing from home only the clothes on our backs. The hem of my skirt was hanging in places and I lingered, letting on I was fixing it. Mr Campbell rapped hard on an old wooden door with his knuckles, and a stern-looking woman in a long dark skirt opened the door.

"Good morning, Matron," he said, trying to be cheerful. "Here are the O'Shea girls, the four of them."

He left us in her care and rushed back to his wife.

"Sit down over there," Matron said firmly, pointing to a large well-scrubbed wooden table.

The room was bare, cold and dismal. Big rusty spoons were put in front of us with bowls of watery soup. I sipped the soup slowly, hating the taste and feel of the rusty spoon in my mouth. The rest of the cutlery was the same – old, bent, rusty and much larger that what we were used to.

After we finished the soup, we were ordered to strip off and get into a giant-sized enamelled bath. We'd never seen such big baths before. Mammy always washed us in a small tin bath in front of the fire.

"Get in and sit down," a cross woman shouted at me.

My bruised, skinny legs struggled over the side as steaming hot water gushed out of its enormous taps. The bath was filled to the top. Her rough hands scrubbed me hard. My head hurt as she vigorously soaped my hair. Terrified, I clung to the sides for fear of drowning in this deep bath of stinging hot water. Feeling red raw, I climbed out and was given a pile of old clothes belonging to the home to put on: a dark pinafore, jersey, fleecy knickers, socks and old shoes. The clothes were shabby and had been worn by other girls in the home. We were separated into our own age groups. I was put with Annie as there was only one year between us.

It was winter, and every morning we were lined up in the cold yard for prayers and Matron's inspection. Two of the women in charge, Miss Cross and Mrs Beatty, stood close by. They were short, thin, hard women with steely grey hair combed well back and pinned up tight. They never smiled or had a kind word to say. When they weren't looking, we'd rub each other's backs to keep warm. These morning inspections were the only times I saw my big sister, Kathleen. One morning at prayers, I heard her ask about Mammy and when we could go home.

"Be quiet," Mrs Beatty snapped, and smacked her across the face.

Kathleen never flinched. She was determined to escape.

"Lily, I'm making plans how to get out. We'll have to climb over those big iron gates," she whispered to me.

That gave me hope.

We were put to work every morning in the bathroom, polishing the copper pipes up and down the walls and under the baths.

"Get under that bath and don't come out till those pipes are shining," Miss Cross would shout, shoving a rag at me.

I squatted close to the other girls under the baths. We whispered as we polished the pipes, warming our hands on them.

Every afternoon we were taken out wearing the home's old navy coats with hats to match. We walked in pairs through the cold, windy streets of Dún Laoghaire. Miss Cross walked in front, her head up straight, and Mrs Beatty walked behind. Local people avoided us and moved over to the other side of the street. On one of these walks, Annie broke a rule. Instead of staying with her partner on the inside path, she walked around a lamp-post, holding on to it. Mrs Beatty's beady eyes never missed a thing. The Birds' Nest's appearances had to be kept up in front of the well-to-do Dún Laoghaire residents. When we arrived back at the home, she thumped my sister hard on the back.

"Don't leave that line again when we're out walking," she warned.

We slept in large dormitories in small iron beds. I longed for our big double bed at home where the four of us slept together, cosy and secure.

When the lights were out, we talked quietly to each other about how horrible the women in charge were.

"They're just like their names, aren't they? Missus Beatty beats us and Miss Cross is always cross."

"We won't be stayin' here long," I said confidently to a girl next to me. "Me mammy's in hospital and me daddy's comin' to take us home soon."

The girl began to sob.

"I've got no one. Me mammy's dead and so's me daddy. I'll never go home."

Worried, I put my head under the sheets and prayed that Daddy would really come and take us all home.

A few weeks later, Matron called us from our individual groups.

"Go to the dining room; your father's there," she said, feigning a smile.

Feeling wanted, Annie and I dropped what we were doing and hurried out. We entered the large cold dining room with its long bare wooden tables. Daddy was standing next to a door at the far end of the room with Kathleen. He tried to cheer us up.

"Jaysus, look at youse. Youse are all dressed the same," he laughed.

We didn't laugh.

"Please, Daddy! Please! Please!" we pleaded. "Take us home, we hate it here!"

"Jesus Christ, I can't," he said, losing his patience. "Yer mammy still isn't well. I promise youse faithfully, I'll take youse home the very next time."

Bending down, he picked up a large paper bag.

"Look what I've brought for youse, luvly oranges!"

We burst out crying when we saw him open the door behind him. Kissing us goodbye, he rushed off. The oranges were taken from us.

Weeks and weeks went by, then one day we were sent to the dining room again. It was Daddy. While my two sisters and I were telling him how badly we were treated, the door burst open and Sylvia was pushed in. As she was only five, she was separated from us in the home. We had nearly forgotten all about her. She ran through the dining room, knocking over chairs, falling and sobbing uncontrollably to get to Daddy quickly.

He rushed over and grabbed her up.

"I'll be back for youse. Youse are all comin' home out a' this feckin' place," he said, his lips tight, his eyes filling up.

A few days later, Matron handed us back the clothes we had arrived in and told us to put them on and go to the dining room where our father was waiting. Matron wasn't smiling; we were supposed to stay longer.

All the way home in the bus, we never stopped talking about the other poor girls we'd left behind with Miss Cross and Mrs Beatty.

Mammy couldn't believe it.

"I thought youse were all happy and being well looked after or I wouldn't have left youse there for so long."

We were only home when Sylvia's golden hair began to fall out, leaving bald patches. Mammy quickly took her to the dispensary. The doctor took one look at her head.

"She's caught ringworm in that home from wearing another child's hat. Her head will have to be shaved. Here's some ointment to rub in."

Mammy put her arm around her.

"Don't worry, love, I'll buy you a nice new flowery bonnet in the bargain stores in Parnell Street to wear while you're playing outside."

After my stay in the Birds' Nest, I shivered whenever I heard Catholic mothers shout at their children, "I swear t'God, youse'll all go to Biddy Smyly's Proddy Home, if youse don't stop it!"

St George's School in
Sherrard Street

Mrs Bradshaw hung her cane on the side of the blackboard as a warning to us all to pay attention. "Wake up, you fool!" she shouted one day to Kathleen, pushing her up against the blackboard.

The heavy blackboard toppled off its easel and fell on Kathleen's shoulder. She screamed in bed that night whenever I moved against her.

"You daughter's collarbone is broken," a doctor from the children's hospital in Temple Street told Mammy next morning. Mammy was shocked.

Mrs Bradshaw denied having caused it.

"It was an accident," she said.

"She can do what she likes with us," Mammy said angrily. "I bet she wouldn't do that to the Darcys."

The Darcys were well off. They had a house all to themselves.

St George's School was a small Protestant school for boys and girls up the age of fourteen. Florrie was my best pal at school. She was a thin, gentle girl with long brown curls and was the only girl in school who wore a school tunic. We played together in the schoolyard and sat next to each other whenever our teacher allowed us.

There were three teachers: a kind elderly gentleman who taught the big boys and girls; my teacher, Mrs Bradshaw, a stout Protestant lady who only smiled when the clergyman came in; and Miss Young, who took the four year olds.

Miss Young would sit on the edge of her table, her long legs crossed, a fur coat wrapped cosily around her and eating a bar of chocolate while she told the four year olds stories. The children would sit staring at her, their mouths watering.

It was the 1940s and a lot of poor children were being sent to school with no breakfast. We thought it was great when the government decided to supply all Dublin schools with free sandwiches, as well as our small bottles of milk. The sandwiches were either cheese, jam or ham. One thing we could be sure of, Protestant or no Protestant, we never got the ham of a Friday.

We had no school bags or books of our own; even our pens, nibs, ink and blotters were supplied by our school. They were all kept safe in Mrs Bradshaw's cupboard and only handed out for lessons. Every year the education department donated a prize to the child with the best handwriting. I would try my hardest to win this prize. Whenever the nib box was passed around, I would search through it for a nib that wasn't bokety, but it didn't make any difference. I still couldn't master the elegant letters like Florrie could.

"You haven't got a hope, *Lil Ní Shéaghdha*," Mrs Bradshaw would say, looking my shoulder. "I think you should practise your Irish."

Irish was compulsory, and we were forced to speak and write certain phrases in this language.

"An bhfuil cead agam ag dul amach, más é do thoil é?" was one sentence we all learnt very quickly. Otherwise Mrs Bradshaw would not have allowed us to go outside to the lavatory.

Mr McCormick, an Irish inspector, came every so often to test our Irish language. On one of his visits, we were sitting in a small group in front of him. He was asking us questions in Irish. I didn't like Irish and soon lost interest. I began to dream about a poem we had just been taught: Padraic Colum's "An Old Woman of the Roads".

> O, to have a little house!
> To own the hearth and stool and all!
> The heaped-up sods upon the fire,
> The pile of turf against the wall.

I wondered what it would be like if we had our own house instead of living in a tenement. Then I thought of Mrs Bradshaw's favourite story, "The Woman Who Lived in the Vinegar Bottle". We must not be greedy and want too much, she'd remind us, or we could end up like the woman in the vinegar bottle, back to where she started. Suddenly, I saw the group looking at me laughing.

"*Lil Ní Shéaghdha! Lil Ní Shéaghdha!*" they shouted.

I stared back at them puzzled, my face red.

Brady, the new boy sitting next to me, nudged my arm.

"It's your ring, Lily," he whispered, pointing to my hand. "The inspector has asked us a question in Irish: 'Which girl in this group is wearing a wedding ring?'"

I glanced at the ring on my finger. It had been Halloween the night before and I had been the lucky one to bite on the piece of barmbrack that had the shiny brass wedding ring. Kathleen was raging. I would be the first to be married in the family.

I was glad it wasn't Mrs Bradshaw who caught me dreaming. Dreamers and latecomers were sure to get the cane.

Sylvia would usually keep me late in the mornings. She had hated school ever since she was in the Bird's Nest.

"Why can't you just say I'm dead?" she'd sob.

"Mammy, will you make her hurry up! I'll get the came for being late," I'd shout back through the tenement hall.

Mammy would come rushing out after me, all the while fixing Sylvia's clothes, making sure everything was well pulled up. And Mammy always waited till I was crossing the road to shout after me, "Lily, are *your* knickers well up?"

I would never look back.

When we arrived at school one morning, the children were standing in a semicircle around the room. They were taking turns reading passages from a large Bible that was being passed along. We were late. Mrs Bradshaw noticed

Sylvia slipping through our room to Miss Young's class.

"Who sewed that patch on your dress?" she demanded, stopping Sylvia.

"My sister Lily did," Sylvia answered, looking around at me.

"*Lil Ní Shéaghdha*, will you please come up here!" Mrs Bradshaw said. "Is that how I taught you to sew patches? Unpick that patch tonight, resew it and show it to me tomorrow."

That afternoon, Sylvia was waiting outside the school gate for me to take her home. I gripped her hand tightly.

"The devil will come to you tonight for making a show of me," I muttered angrily. "And if you tell on me again, I'll blow feathers at you."

I knew Sylvia was terrified of the devil, and she'd scream at loose feathers flying around the room when Mammy was recovering our pillows. She thought the feathers were alive. That night she slept with her head hidden under the blankets and pillow. Mammy was angry with me next morning.

"Lily, I'm fed up with you giving out about Missus Bradshaw. Maybe I should listen to Mister McManus and send youse all to a Catholic school."

Mr McManus, our St Vincent de Paul man, had been trying to persuade Mammy for ages to change our school. He came with another man most weeks and would sit for hours, talking about her money worries and the obligations she had to fulfil in being married to a Catholic. I would sit listening.

"You know, Missus O'Shea," he'd say seriously, "you are in a mixed marriage, and it would please your husband no end if you sent the children to a Catholic school. It would be the makings of him."

Mammy finally agreed when he handed her a food voucher and a promise of raincoats to come. Opening the door of our room to leave, Mr McManus looked back at me and smiled.

"That young wan talks with her eyes, Missus O'Shea. I wish you'd let me send her down the country to my parents. She'd get a good education."

Mammy just laughed.

It was our first day in this huge Catholic school in Gardiner Street. My sisters and I stood nervously in the crowded playground. Children screamed with laughter as they chased around, knocking each other over and banging into us.

We felt lost. There seemed to be thousands of children and we knew none of them. A bell rang and they all charged towards the doors, pushing and shoving. The teacher looked above their heads and shouted something in Irish. A straight line was formed and we all marched in.

The classes were huge and noisy. The bold boys, sitting in the back, recognised me from Fitzgibbon Street.

"Ya're a Protestant. Why aren't ya going t'yer own school?" they said, as they swapped their ragged comics.

I bit my lip and wished I were sitting next to Florrie.

The teacher was in a world of her own. She banged her cane off the blackboard in time to the loud chanting of tables and spellings.

I thought of my own Protestant school: how Mrs Bradshaw always rewarded me for my tables and spellings. She would allow me to go to her cupboard and take out her picture-card viewer. I'd gaze through the viewer, enjoying the softness of the brown velvet rims of the lenses against my eyes. After sliding in one of her scenery cards, I'd move the magnifying glass backwards and forwards to focus it. In the silence of Mrs Bradshaw's classroom, I would be taken to the snowy mountains of Switzerland or the jungles of Africa.

A bell rang.

It was the end of the day in this Catholic school. We all stood up and said prayers to Mary. We didn't sing "God Save

Our Gracious King". The teacher dismissed us. The children charged towards the door.

We were only in this school for a short time. Mr Campbell soon had us all back in our small Protestant school again – and just in time too. It was end of the year. Mrs Bradshaw always passed around a tin of expensive toffees for us all to take one.

DADDY RYAN

D addy Ryan, our school inspector, had a full-time job chasing after the hundreds of children who were continuously absent from schools around the city. He was a short, stocky, red-faced man with flat feet. Whenever I was late for school, I'd see him panting along the North Circular Road, stopping occasionally to dab his sweaty face with his hanky.

Jesus, there's Daddy Ryan, I'd think to myself, recognising his grey pin-striped suit. *I wonder which school he's going to?*

Everyone knew that Daddy Ryan went around the schools collecting the names of children who were absent. With his long list of names, he would visit their homes to warn their parents that if their children continued to miss school they would be sent to a home.

I hope he's not after Florrie. She hasn't been coming to school again. Mrs Bradshaw said she's sick.

But Daddy Ryan was mainly after the boys who were mitching. They would be hiding down the canals looking for pinkeens or throwing stones in the water.

Not all the children who were absent from school were

mitching. Some were kept home because they were very sick or had nothing to wear. Betty from the Barrack Lane frequently missed school because she had only one shabby dress, no coat and sometimes no shoes to wear.

Others were kept home to mind their younger brothers and sisters. Our neighbour, Mrs Carroll, who lived opposite, thought nothing of keeping her little girl out of school.

"Sure, God love her, she hates school anyway, so I let her stay home to mind the babby," Mrs Carroll would tell Mammy.

Fathers were soft hearted with their favourites.

"Paddy's not t'go t'school today," Mr Murphy would shout back upstairs to Mrs Murphy. "It's lashing rain. Leave him be."

Daddy Ryan always looked footsore as he traipsed from street to street, in and out of tenements, banging off room doors.

Doors weren't always opened.

"If Paddy continues to miss school, he'll end up in Artane," Daddy Ryan would shout through Murphy's keyhole.

After hiding Paddy under the bed, Mrs Murphy would open the door, act shocked and surprised. She would nod in agreement.

"Now, isn't dat a terrible young fella, Mister Ryan? I'll murder him when I get him home. Honest t'God, I will!"

As soon as Daddy Ryan was out of sight, Paddy would reappear. And rain or no rain, he'd be sent out for the messages.

MY WINTER OVERCOAT

Coming home from school one day, I was surprised to see Mammy standing outside the hall door of our tenement. I ran across the road as she came down the steps to meet me.

"Listen, Lily," she said excitedly, rubbing my cold bare arms up and down, "I want you to go and see Missus McNeill. I have given her Robbie's old laundry coat. She's going to turn it inside out and make it into a lovely coat for you for the winter."

"Oh no," I moaned, "not that awful black coat you put over us in bed."

Robbie was working in the Phoenix Laundry. He was a delivery boy and had to sit up high behind two big working horses on a huge laundry cart from early morning to late at night. He had just been issued with a new overcoat. It was made of coarse, heavy black material to protect him from the cold winter rain, snow and sleet. And now I was to get his old coat!

"You'd better hurry, Lily. Missus McNeill wants to measure you. You'll need a coat before it gets really cold. You know her house; it's just across the square."

I had often heard Mammy talk about Mrs McNeill from our parish. She was living apart from her husband with her two children.

"She's a great dressmaker," Mammy'd say, "and such a hard worker. She works on her sewing machine from early morning to late at night."

Mrs McNeill lived in a small room at the top of a quiet tenement house in Great Denmark Street. When I arrived, the hall door was closed over. A man pushed in front of me, kicked the door open and ran ahead up the stairs, his long legs taking two steps at a time. My feet dragged behind me as the stairs narrowed. Mrs McNeill's son, George, let me in. I noticed his dark curly hair and his short trousers with braces looped over his jersey. He was my age.

"Mammy will see you in a minute," he said, pointing to his mother who was hunched up over a sewing machine that rested on a large table.

The table was cluttered with piles of old clothes. George sat back down at one corner where his school books were laid out and continued writing.

I wonder what he's writing? I thought to myself. I knew they were Protestants, and I was puzzled why he didn't go to my school. Mrs Bradshaw never let us take our exercise books home.

Mrs McNeill didn't look up but continued sewing. I stared around her small dreary room at the dark corners and shadows. I could barely see the outline of two single beds. Clothes hung untidily on each of the brass knobs. An oil lamp flickered near by. The man that had run ahead of me on the stairs was sitting on the table next to Mrs McNeill, his legs dangling. Half-made garments lay under the table on the bare wooden floor. A little curly haired blonde girl sat at her feet, humming and playing with the bits of old rags that her mother dropped from time to time.

Feeling tired, I moved from foot to foot. After a while Mrs McNeill stood up and measured me. She was a tall, thin lady with large brown weary eyes, who didn't talk to you and ask lots of questions about Mammy and all, like the other women in our street did.

"Can you come back next week for a fitting?" was the only question she asked.

When I arrived the following week, it was the same. George let me in, returned to the table and continued with his writing. Mrs McNeill was busily sewing and little Phoebe was playing on the floor with scraps of rags. And that man was sitting close to her again talking quietly. Whenever her long dark hair fell down from its hair pins, he'd pin it back up again. She looked flushed and happy. He took a bar of chocolate from his pocket, broke off a square and popped it in her mouth, and than popped one in his own.

"Khh, khh," I coughed. My habit cough.

Mrs McNeill looked around and reassured me that she would not be long.

"She leaves me waiting for ages while she talks to that man," I whinged to Mammy that evening.

"Oh," Mammy said slowly, "I think I know who he is. He works across the road from her in offices. He's younger than her. Ah well, I suppose she gets lonely."

When the coat was finished, Mrs McNeill put it on me, picked all the bits of fluff out of the seams and asked me to turn around.

"Now, doesn't that look grand!" she said, brushing the coat down with her hand. "You'll be nice and warm for the winter."

I didn't feel grand in Robbie's old laundry coat that weighed me down to the ground, and I couldn't see much difference. It still looked like a man's coat, except it was now turned inside out, a bit shorter and had a small vent at the back – that stuck out. I felt my face burn when George glanced over at me.

Every morning I grumbled bitterly as my fingers struggled to push the large buttons through the stiff buttonholes. The coarseness of the material rubbed against my neck and the insides of my legs, and it still had the smell of horses from Robbie's laundry cart. But worst of all, boys from my school began to shout after me, "Lily's wearing her daddy's coat! Lily's wearing her daddy's coat!"

Running home, I would throw the coat on the bed and burst out crying.

Mammy eventually lost her temper, grabbed hold of me and the coat and dragged me back to school. Straight into the classroom she went, where Mrs Bradshaw was cleaning the blackboard with a duster. She pleaded with her to speak to the boys who were calling after me.

"Missus O'Shea," Mrs Bradshaw said, in a cold, firm voice, "I'm afraid Lily will just have to take it. She will have to learn not to be so thin skinned."

FLORRIE

"**M**ammy, Florrie's dead!" I shouted, running in from school. "Missus Bradshaw told us. I t'ink it must a' been her cough that killed her!"

"Ah God, no, is she? God love her," Mammy said, sitting down.

After a few minutes, Mammy jumped up, went over to the fire, grabbed the poker and began to rake the ashes out vigorously.

I went over and stood beside her.

"Mammy, why didn't Florrie's mammy hold her head over the hot steaming tar when the Corporation was fixing the roads, like other mothers do, then she might have got better?"

"No, that's only for whooping cough. I think poor Florrie had TB," Mammy said sadly. "Don't forget and say a prayer for her tonight."

Florrie didn't have a sister to play with and would ask me back to her home. She had three brothers, two older and one younger, who also went to our school. Her mammy didn't let her play in the street because she was too delicate.

Holding hands after school, we'd skip happily down the North Circular Road to her home. Horses and carts would be rumbling by on this busy road.

"Let's look in here," I'd say, pulling her over to a stone horse trough at the edge of the kerb.

It was great when a horse would stop for a drink. The driver, with his greasy flat cap, would sit sucking his butt, staring in front of him, patiently waiting till his horse was satisfied. Fascinated, we'd stare at the horse's huge tongue, slobbering with froth and spit as it lapped up the water. But we'd soon hurry on when the horse would decide to relieve itself, sending gallons of hot steaming urine gushing down the edge of the kerb.

Florrie lived on the North Circular Road, right at the bottom of my street. Her home, a converted loft, was behind two old wooden gates that hung crookedly in between a row of tenement houses. Laughing excitedly, we'd push one gate ajar and squeeze into a large cobblestoned yard that had several stables. This was the only bit of spare land between all these tenements. Chickens and hens would be strutting around, their small heads bobbing up and down pecking seeds. Several fat pigs would be slobbering away in a pigsty. Florrie's two big brothers would swish it out, throwing in bucket after bucket of water. Shrieking happily, we'd chase each other around her yard, sending the chickens scurrying for cover.

"C'mon, Lily," Florrie would laugh, leading me up narrow wooden steps to a door that opened up to a large cosy room that had once been a loft over the stables. Their lavatory and the tap for their water were down in the yard.

Her mammy was a big countrywoman. I never saw Florrie's daddy.

"Come in our of the cold, girls, and sit yourselves down by the fire," she'd say in her soft brogue.

A big tea of fried bacon and black and white pudding

would be quickly cooked; all of this and a whole egg would be placed on a thick crispy piece of fried bread and put in front of me.

"I only ever get a whole egg at Easter," I'd say, sitting down at the table.

Florrie's mammy would ask me questions about our family while she cooked tea for her big boys. I'd jump up to go when I'd see her open the door to call them up for tea.

"I'll see ya across that road, love. It's very busy at this time," Florrie's mammy would say, leading me down the wooden steps from the loft.

After Florrie died, I felt sad. I knew I'd miss her and the visits to her home. Her yard was what I imagined a farm in the country to be like. Most of all, I'd miss her mother's warm homely kitchen and the sound of her pan sizzling as she fried our sausages, bacon and black and white pudding. And I couldn't boast about it to my sisters any more.

Not long after her, Florrie's younger brother died too. I was used to people dying and just accepted it, and said a prayer, like Mammy told me to.

THE ROYAL CANAL

"Look! There's somebody down there in the water drowned," a boy called out to me, pointing into the canal with a stick.

The boy was under an archway of the Royal Canal peering down at something in the water. I never liked going under the archways – they stank of urine and felt cold and damp – but I was curious. I left my pals and ran under the bridge to see what he was looking at. Leaning over the edge, I could see a boy lying still on the mossy mud at the bottom of the canal. He was wearing black bathing nicks. His pale, white body glared up at me. It was late evening, the sun had gone down and the smelly archway was more frightening.

"Someone that knows him has gone for his mammy," the boy said calmly.

Just then I heard a noise, turned round and saw a couple of barefoot boys running in our direction.

"He's over here, Missus! In the water under the bridge," they shouted back to a stout, red-faced woman who was struggling to keep up with them.

The woman's floral apron was flapping around her, and her flat, unfastened shoes click-clacked as she panted towards us. When she started screaming, I ran away and caught up with my pals who were gone walking on home. I tried not to hear the mother's cries behind me, but I did. I had nightmares for weeks after.

The Royal Canal was not far from where I lived and I often went down there. On warm sunny days, boys jumped off the locks into the dirty canal water. It was not unusual to see bare bums disappear under the murky water. City boys taught themselves how to swim this way. Dodging around filthy rubbish, planks of wood and bloated sacks with dead cats and dogs inside, they'd splash and doggy-paddle over to the edge, climb up and jump off the lock again.

During the school holidays, crowds of children flocked to the canals. Parts of our canal had high grassy embankments that sloped down to a narrow path close to the edge of the water. We would roll down on the large mounds and make endless chains from the abundance of daisies that grew there. Mothers smiled happily at us as they strolled along pushing their laden prams.

I'd have so many things to tell Mammy when I got home.

"Mammy, a boy took a fit today by the canal. He was up on

one of the embankments. He rolled around on the grass with spits comin' out of his mouth. His brothers stood around him, makin' sure he didn't fall into the water."

"God help him," Mammy said.

"An', Mammy, d'ya know those two white swans that swim up an' down in the canal with their heads up in the air? Well they're now hidin' in that part where the tall, skinny reeds grow. Everybody says that they're layin' eggs, and they're in a bad mood."

Mammy nodded and went on cutting up a loaf of bread for our tea. We'd eat the bread quicker than she could cut it.

Mammy was always interested in our news and would repeat it to the women at the hall door that evening.

"For God's sake, be careful on those locks," she'd warn us when she'd hear from Mrs Murphy that we'd been on them.

But my pals and I could never pass the locks without wanting to cross them. We'd follow the other children on to the rickety wooden plank and cling tightly to the only support there was – a single iron rail. The lock would creak and sway. Hardly daring to look down at the depth of the water (none of us could swim), we would squeal with excitement and terror as we hurried to the safety of the other side of the canal.

Sometimes we would be lucky enough to be passing just as the lock-keeper opened the locks. We'd dash to the edge to watch the water gush down from one side to the other until it was level. A flat wooden barge would chug through. In the boats, the men wearing big rubber boots always looked cranky and never waved back.

Even though Mammy forbade Johnny to go down the canal, he still went every chance he got, poking sticks in and looking for pinkeens. I was outside playing one Sunday when I saw a group of strange boys leading him up our street from the direction of the canal. A couple of them were running in front. Now and again they'd glance back at my brother who was soaking wet, his boots squelching as he walked. A big boy in patched short trousers held up by braces was walking in his bare feet next to Johnny. I ran ahead of them as fast as I could into our room and called out to Mammy.

"Mammy, it's Johnny! He's been down the canal again and some boys are bringin' him up the street. Wait till ya see his good jacket. It's wringin' wet."

"Jeesus!" Mammy cried, dropping the blanket off our bed that she'd been examining. She rushed out after me into the street.

The big boy pushed my brother forward.

"He nearly drownded, Missus, but I jumped in and saved him," he said proudly.

Johnny just stood there, his head down, water dripping off him. He looked white and shocked.

"What in the name a' God was he doing?" Mammy said, whipping his jacket off.

"He was throwin' stones in the water, Missus, and threw himself in instead."

Still shaking with fright, Mammy brought the boys into our room and gave them all the only thing she could afford – a thick slice of bread and butter with sugar sprinkled on it. They left happily with their reward. Johnny was stripped off and scrubbed very hard with Lifebuoy soap in a basin of water, hair and all. He sat in the armchair shivering, eating a piece of bread and butter, swearing to Mammy that he'd never go down the canal again. But of course he did.

ME PRAM'S NEVER EMPTY

Just as often as there were deaths in the tenements, there were births. New babies were being born all the time. The proud mothers would go around the neighbours showing off their new babies. Mammy was always pleased when they'd knock on our door.

"I thought you might like to see me new little babby, Missus O'Shea," our neighbour Mrs Carroll said one day. "I've just had her christened and I've had me blessing too."

She gently pulled back the lacy cream wool shawl which her baby was wrapped in.

"Ah, God love her. Isn't she lovely?" Mammy said, opening her purse and putting something into the baby's tiny hand.

I squeezed in front of Mammy to get a peep at the baby's long white christening robe and its fancy satin bonnet with flowing ribbons. It didn't seem to matter how poor the mothers were, they would have their babies dressed up in the best christening clothes they could lay their hands on.

"And how old are these?" Mammy smiled, looking down at Mrs Carroll's other little ones.

"Well, he's just out a' the pram, Missus, God love him, an' she's nearly three. Ah, sure me pram's never empty. But God's good, he never sends a mouth without food for it."

It would not be long though before the new baby would be tucked up in the pram outside our neighbour's tenement, the handle tied firmly to the railings with a bit of old string or the daddy's tie.

Wanting to play mothers, my pals and I would knock on room doors and ask if we could mind their new baby. We'd race for the door where we knew there was a pram without bockety wheels or baby sick.

Off we'd go, wheeling the prams down Belvedere, past St

George's Church, on into Dorset Street and up towards Drumcondra. We loved Drumcondra Road; it was park-like with its wide path and tall shady trees. We'd sit down on the first available seat watching the traffic go by to the city. Whenever the babies made a whimper, we'd shake the prams, shove the soothers into their mouths and sing:

> Oh, I'll never forget the day that I was born.
> It was in the winter, on a cold and frosty morn.
> The nurse, she washed me all over,
> And covered me little bum to keep it warm.
> Then she rocked me in a cra-dle,
> In the little shirt me mudder made for me.

If they didn't stop crying, we'd lift them out of their warm prams, pull up our jerseys and let on to breastfeed them. Many a baby was nearly dropped.

CHRISTMAS PARTIES

Every year, the lord mayor of Dublin, Alfie Byrne, gave a Christmas party for the poor and needy children around the city. The party was held in the Mansion House where the lord mayor resided. The St Vincent de Paul men had the hard task of distributing the tickets fairly among the many Catholic families who lived in the tenements.

One night our Vincent de Paul men brought us four lovely new raincoats with souwesters to match, all different colours. One of the men, Mr McManus, was extra kind and gave Mammy a few spare tickets for Alfie Byrne's Christmas party as well. We had heard about this great party in the Mansion

House from other children in the street, but this year, 1939, was the first time we received tickets.

Although excited, I felt a bit afraid. I wanted to go but was not sure where the Mansion House was. I knew it was somewhere on the south side, where all the grand shops and posh people were.

"You and Annie go, and take Sylvia with youse," Mammy said, "and when youse are crossing a big road, ask some woman to see youse across. Do youse hear me?"

It was a cold December day when we set out to make our way to the party. Holding Sylvia's hand, Annie and I hurried along down O'Connell Street. When we crossed over O'Connell Bridge, an icy wind blew up from the Liffey between the pillars, biting into our legs and faces and making them red and sore. I held my new red satin raincoat tightly around me and felt pleased Mammy had insisted that we wear our warm pixie hoods. Sylvia started to cry and wanted to go back home.

"Ya're all right," I told her crossly, as we dragged her across the bridge towards Trinity College. "Ya have yer buttoned-up gaiters on yer legs, haven't ya? We'll be at the party soon."

Passing the closed iron gates of Trinity College, we remembered Mammy's instructions to keep to the railings and follow it right around till we came to Dawson Street. We noticed groups of children on the far side of the street. Some of them had their little sisters or brothers with them.

"They must be going to the party," Sylvia said, brightening up.

We ran across the road and followed them up Dawson Street into a wide driveway.

"That must be the Mansion House," I said, pointing to a large, two-storey Georgian house with six long windows on each side of the door.

Crowds of children stood on the concrete steps that led up to its big wooden door. We squeezed in amongst them and tried to ignore the pushing and shoving. We were all eager to get into the party and out of the cold. We finally got to the entrance and were relieved to see a properly formed queue going inside this magnificent house. Men who looked important stood around directing us towards a huge room that led off its large hall. This room, with its beautiful ornate ceiling, had lots of long tables laid out with plates of sandwiches and cakes. The men tried hard to be heard above the children's loud, excited voices as they led us to a table to take some food. Hands were pushing in from every direction grabbing the cakes.

"Get me a cake! Get me a cake!" Sylvia cried.

"Keep moving! Keep moving!" a loud voice shouted from behind. "There are others waiting outside to come in."

We moved slowly out of the room towards a door that led outside. Some of the boys were stuffing small cakes into their pockets as they went. Close to the door stood two young, smartly dressed ladies behind a small table. They were chatting and laughing together. As we walked by them, they automatically handed each one of us a small bag of sweets, one big shiny red apple and an orange.

When we arrived home, the door of our room was open. Mammy was on her knees scrubbing the floorboards. She brushed back her hair and stared up at us.

"My God, that was a quick party if ever I saw one!"

Soon after Alfie Byrnes' party, my sisters and I went to another Christmas party. This party was organised every year by Mr Campbell for all the boys and girls of our school. It was always held in our parish hall next door to St George's Church. Mammy made us take Johnny. She put his good grey blazer on him, washed his face and combed his hair.

We were early and ran up the stairs nervously and into the hall. Colourful Christmas chains decorated the ceiling of this long narrow room. Close to the stage was the most wonderful

Christmas tree imaginable. Small unwrapped toys, some second-hand, were resting on its thick, green branches.

"Let's slide up and down while we're waiting for the party to begin," I said excitedly.

The highly wax-polished floor was great for sliding on. Now and again, we stopped and gazed at the Christmas tree, wondering what present we'd get.

Would Mr Campbell give us that lovely coloured ball, or that game that looked like Ludo? Maybe Johnny might get that fire engine with the key.

There were lots of other small presents on the tree, like paint sets, little pink gelatine dolls and whistles.

Mr Campbell, dressed as usual in his clerical clothes, stood quietly by, smiling.

Several stout ladies were busy making sandwiches and setting out plates of small, delicious, pyramid-shaped iced cakes on a long wooden table. When we were all seated, they bustled around us, pouring out cups of sweet milky tea, making sure that no child was left out. After we'd eaten, two of the ladies gathered us together; one played the piano and sang, while the other organised games.

Every year, I had envied the girls at this party who wore bright-coloured party dresses – especially when we were playing "London Bridge Is Falling Down" and "Oranges and Lemons". Holding my partner's hand to form an arch, I would watch these girls skip down the hall, their beautiful satin party dresses billowing out, and I longed for one.

But this year was different. I didn't have to wear my jersey and winter skirt. Mammy had found a pink silk nightdress in a parcel of old clothes that had been given to her. I begged her to shorten it and make it into a party dress for me. My dress didn't billow out when I swung around, but I didn't care, as long as it had the big puffed sleeves and a wide sash tied in a large bow at the back. It was just like a real party dress.

After the games, Mr Campbell called out our names one at a time to come up and receive a present from the tree. Those of us who never missed Sunday school received a brand new book as well.

We ran all the way home to show Mammy our presents. I knew I'd have great fun with my puzzle book. One of my makey-up games in bed was "Guess the Word". I'd choose a word in my old book, jumble up the letters and call them out. After the person guessed the word, they'd take the book and have a go. Sometimes the book even went flying across the room to the boys' bed. Now that I had a new book, I could try out different words on my brothers and sisters.

Kathleen sat in the armchair reading her book of fairy tales. Annie searched the mantlepiece for the scissors to cut out her dress-up paper doll. Sylvia hugged her ball.

"Who got the mouth organ?" Mammy laughed, looking at Johnny. "I heard youse coming a mile away."

CHRISTMAS IN THE TENEMENTS

As a child, it puzzled me why Mammy worried so much about the success of her Christmas pudding. We would not have minded what it looked like, we just loved the taste of it.

"Oh, please God it hasn't stuck to the cloth," she'd say anxiously.

We'd all hold our breath as she untied the string. To our relief and delight, the pudding would drop on to the plate with a perfect smooth skin all over it.

Mammy tried hard to make our Christmases happy. The making of the Christmas pudding was a happy occasion in itself. But this year was a difficult year: Granny had died, and Mammy missed Granny's few-bob pension. She went to Mr Campbell for help. He gave her a note for Blake's in Meath Street to get the makings of her pudding.

"God, if it wasn't for him we'd have nothing, no pudding or anything," she said, looking at the note.

While playing outside a few hours later, we spotted Mammy coming down our street struggling with her shopping bag. We ran up and took the heavy bag from her.

"I hope you got some broken biscuits, an', Mammy, when are you makin' the puddin'?" I said, following her through the tenement hall.

"Give me a chance to take my hat and coat off, for God's sake!" she said, collapsing in a chair.

We sat around the table as Mammy emptied the loose fruit into a basin.

"Here, Lily," she said, "you can start taking the stones out of the raisins and sultanas, while I shred up the suet."

My sisters and I laughed and fooled around, our hands becoming sticky from squeezing the stones out. Mammy worked on, doing all the hard jobs: chopping up the large lumps of green and orange candied peel and crumbing the stale heels of bread into a big mound. Before she mixed all the ingredients together, she cracked the eggs into a bowl, beating them up thoroughly with one of our old forks. I loved the strong smell of spices that drifted up from the bowl as she poured the bottle of stout in.

We all lined up happily to stir the mixture three times to make our wish.

Mammy gritted her teeth as she tied the string of the pudding up as tight as she could in a cloth that had been boiled, greased and floured. She would sprinkle flour over the knot to make a flour bung, then tie another knot to hold the flour in. This would help to keep the water out. The pudding gurgled away for hours in our big iron pot on the glowing red-hot coal. Mr Campbell always sent us coal at Christmas. The smell of the boiled fruit and spices floated around the room as Mammy lifted the pudding out of the pot. We watched her as she quickly stuck a meat hook under the string. The butcher had given her this hook to hang her pudding up with.

"Will youse all stop smelling the pudding, for God's sake, and help me. Lily, will you take me coat down off the back of the door and throw it over the end of me bed," Mammy said, holding up the steaming hot pudding.

There was a big round stain on the back of our door from the constant bumping of our Christmas pudding as we ran in and out of our room till Christmas.

And another bit of luck came our way that year. Mammy's friend from the parish had been sent a huge fat turkey from her wealthy relatives in the country. Her friend could not face the messy job of removing its head, plucking the feathers and cleaning out its insides, so she gave it to Mammy. It was the first Christmas we ever had a turkey.

Our parish was small and most of the parishioners were well-to-do. They were generous and passed on their old toys to the poor of our parish at Christmas. Mr Campbell gave Mammy an address for her to collect a parcel of old toys from one of these parishioners. She let on to us that it was only a parcel of old clothes and quickly stuffed it under her bed. Later on, she dropped a hint that I might receive a boy doll for Christmas. Crawling around under her bed, I found this doll.

Annie saw me.

"Mammy, Lily's after seein' a doll under yer bed," she shouted, looking pleased with herself.

Mammy was angry.

"What were you doing crawling under my bed? I told youse not to!"

95

"We were only playin'. I didn't really see anyt'in'. I'll forget all about it now."

Christmas Eve came and my sisters and I were eager to get to bed early. We hung up our stockings on the brass knobs at the end of our bed. I already had a name for my boy doll: Billy Boy.

Outside in the street, we could hear the sound of men coming home drunk. Drawn to the window, I peeped out and tried hard not to be seen. Some men were merry and singing at the top of their voices, but others were in a dark mood, swearing at passers-by, looking for a fight. They staggered by our window, grabbing hold of our railings to try and steady themselves.

Mr Murphy appeared on our tenement steps. He was dragging along a big stuffed pancake-faced doll – nearly the size of his daughter Mary.

Inside our room, Mammy was busy rushing around preparing our bath in front of the fire.

"Come away from that window!" she called out.

We all stripped off to our vests and knickers and stood around our small tin bath shivering, waiting our turn to be washed. Johnny had already been washed and was sitting in our big armchair in his clean nightshirt looking at one of his old comics. Robbie was working late. One by one, we sat in the bath while Mammy scrubbed us; then we knelt by the fire in our clean vests and knickers till our hair dried.

Suddenly there was a loud knock on our door.

"Quick, get into bed till I see who it is," Mammy whispered, shoving the bath to one side.

We made a mad dash for the bed. Several boys from the Boy's Brigade struggled in carrying a large Christmas hamper. Mammy quickly closed the door so as not to let all the heat out. Placing the hamper on the table, the boys wished us a happy Christmas and then rushed out into the cold, wintry night air.

A large Christmas cake was only one of the delights in that hamper. How lovely it looked, wrapped in its bright red paper with sprigs of green holly painted all over it! The cake was passed around immediately, so that each one of us could smell and inhale its spicy fragrance.

"Oh God, aren't they very good," Mammy said, taking out tea, butter and sugar.

"An' look, Mammy? There's a big bag of Jacob biscuits," I said, kneeling up on the chair, going through the hamper.

"Now, get inta bed, all of youse. Father Christmas will be here soon," Mammy said, lowering the gas globe.

I woke up that night to see Daddy arranging soldiers on the top of a toy fort next to the bed where Robbie and Johnny slept. I lay there quietly watching him, letting on to be asleep.

I never forgot this scene.

Next morning, Kathleen found her knickers pegged to the end of our bed with something in it.

"Santa Claus wanted to give you a game, Kathleen, but your stocking wasn't big enough," Mammy said seriously.

We all laughed and laughed.

Our stockings were full of surprises: an apple, an orange and small games of snakes and ladders. Johnny, still in his nightshirt, was playing with his soldiers. Annie got an old-fashioned doll's pram. She never let this pram out of her sight. Even at night, she slept on the outside of our bed holding on tightly to the bone handle of the pram for fear that I might get up in the night and have a wheel of it.

Annie got the pram, but where was my Billy Boy?

"I didn't get my doll, Mammy," I said, trying to keep back the tears.

Mammy said nothing. She went on plucking the turkey.

"Where's me doll, Mammy?" I said again.

"You might get it later," she said as she continued preparing the stuffing for the turkey.

After chopping the fresh parsley, sage and thyme, Mammy added a chopped onion and breadcrumbs. She mixed all this together with a pinch of salt and melted butter, then squeezed it into the turkey and sewed it up with a needle and thread – just like she did with the cow's heart we had most weeks.

The church bells were merrily ringing, both Protestant and Catholic. Somehow the bells seemed to be louder than usual. Outside our window, we could hear women chatting as they rushed by on their way to early mass. Robbie was gone to pump the organ at our church. Mammy had lit the big red candle that Miss Flynn from the dairy had given her for nothing. It stood in a saucer on the mantelpiece. The fire was lighting, and even the slop bucket had been emptied.

Miss Munroe knocked on our door to take us to church. Daddy was snoring; his coat was quickly pulled up over his head. Into our room she came, carrying four white boxes. Every Christmas, Miss Munroe gave my sisters and me a beautiful doll each. I opened my box very carefully. The box, with its shiny silver lace trim, was a treasure in itself. The doll's dress was a pretty pastel colour with a frilled bonnet to match, and on her feet she wore little silver shoes and white socks. Each doll was dressed in a different colour. But the dolls' heads were fragile and broke on the first fall, so it wouldn't be long before we'd all be nursing half-headed dolls.

Carrying our dolls proudly, we hurried up the Barrack Lane to Charles Street and our church. Other children were playing with their new toys in the street. Many were on their way to mass, wheeling their brand new dolls' prams that left trails in the soft, falling sleet.

On arriving home from church, Mammy gave me Black
Billy Boy – dressed complete in a perfect little man's striped
shirt, braces and trousers – and for the rest of Christmas day
I sang to him:

> I had a little nigger
> And he wouldn't grow any bigger,
> So I put him in the winder
> For a show.
> He pulled down the winder,
> And broke his little finger,
> Then couldn't play his old banjo.

As a child, I couldn't see any harm in this song. Only years
later did I become aware of the hurtful names we called
people and the insensitive songs we sang.

THE SLOP BUCKET

Aunt Sheila, a small plump woman with fair curly hair
and bright blue eyes, came to visit us one day. She
came to ask Mammy if I could go and look after her
three small children.

"You don't mind, Dolly, do you? I just want to slip out on
me own for a couple of hours."

I was nine years old and felt big and important when
Mammy agreed.

I didn't know Aunt Sheila that well. Her visits were rare.
Whenever she did come, she'd stand in the middle of the
room and refuse to sit down.

"I can't stay long, Dolly. I can't stay long," she'd repeat in between asking after Daddy. Her children clung to her coat. Although they weren't that much younger than us, they acted babyish, at least that's what Mammy said.

Sheila, the eldest, was eight; Laura was seven; and Billy was five. Mammy thought young Sheila looked like me, skinny with short brown hair; and she thought Laura and Billy were the image of their mammy with their fair curly hair.

"I must get ready to go," I said early next morning.

Grabbing our kettle, I rushed out into the yard to fill it. Several women had come downstairs with the slop buckets and were struggling across the yard to the lavatory to empty them. I went and stood behind the women who were waiting at the tap to fill their kettles. Our black iron kettle felt terribly heavy as I carried it in. I almost dropped it. I poured some water from it into our chipped enamelled basin. Mammy had put the basin on a chair for me to wash. Dipping the corner of the towel into the cold water, I scrubbed my face and neck.

"C'mere to me," Mammy said smiling, as she reached up for the comb on the mantelpiece. "I'll put a ribbon in your hair."

My sisters, still in their vests, were sitting up in bed watching me enviously. With a clean dress on and my runners whitened, I skipped off down the steps of the tenements and ran up our street towards Mountjoy Square. I dawdled down Hutton's Lane past the butcher who always joked with Mammy whenever she was buying pig's cheek.

"I've left the *eye* in it to see you through the week, Missus O'Shea," he'd say with a wry grin, wrapping it up in paper.

I hurried on into Parnell Street and peeped into Kennedy's bakery. The hot, steamy smell of freshly baked bread sailed out to me. Aunt Sheila, Daddy's favourite sister, lived over a small sweetshop on the other side of this busy street. Horses and carts carrying heavy loads rode up and down. Dealers with makeshift stalls stood all along the edge of the footpath on the opposite side. Old hoodless prams, jammed packed with empty wooden orange boxes, were next to the dealers. I waited until it was safe to dash across. It was Friday and the dealers were busy.

"Get yer herrin's and fresh mackerels!" they sang out loudly.

Their hands looked red and swollen as they gutted their fish and threw the insides into a tin bucket beside them.

I stopped outside the sweetshop where my aunt lived in a room above. I stared into the shop's sparkling clean window. They didn't have any fizz-bags with the jelly lollypops inside or red Nancy balls like McClean's in our street sold, but there were jars and jars of all different kinds of sweets – including my favourites, acid drops and Mickey Mouse toffee. My mouth watered as I stood wondering which of these sweets I would buy with the penny I hoped Aunt Sheila'd give me. There was a large chocolate box in the window with a picture of an old-fashioned lady wearing a wide frilled bonnet on the lid.

Wouldn't it be great, I thought, *if I could buy that chocolate box.*

I pushed my aunt's hall door in and climbed the dark, narrow wooden stairs to her room above the shop.

"Come on in, Lily. Just let me wash me face and comb me hair."

I stood beside the children while she fussed around looking for her garters. Sighing, she put on her old lisle stockings, pulled them up to just above the knee and then twisted a farthing around the rim at the top to tighten and hold them up. Mammy did this when she mislaid her garters, and it fascinated me. In no time at all, Aunt Sheila was ready.

"Cheerio, I won't be long," she called back, reaching for her coat hanging on a nail at the back of the door.

There were no toys to be seen, not even a doll with a broken head. Wondering what game to play with my cousins, I looked around at the large heavy furniture in this small room.

There were lots of dark corners where we could hide: a tall, deep cupboard to slip into, my aunt and uncle's big bed to crawl under and an iron cot that we could climb behind.

"Let's play hide-and-seek," I said.

The children jumped up and down laughing, happy and eager to join in the game with me. Time sped by. They laughed and squealed each time I found them in my aunt's cupboard, and clothes were going everywhere.

When it was my turn to hide, I slipped in behind my aunt's long lace curtains. My foot got caught and I tripped and fell, knocking over her slop bucket that she hid there.

My heart pounded with fright as I looked helplessly at the empty bucket and the dirty, smelly somethin' running all over her well-scrubbed floor.

"Mammy'll murder ya," said little Sheila with a frightened pale face.

She quickly ran and found me a piece of old rag that her mammy used as a floor cloth. I was on my hands and knees trying to mop it up when Aunt Sheila walked in.

"Sacred Heart a' Jesus! Look at the mess a' me place," she cried out in a low whining voice as she collapsed into a chair.

Leaving the floor cloth and the bucket, I jumped up and hurried over to the cupboard, trying to push back the clothes that had tumbled out. The children, seeing their mammy upset, got out of her way. They ran under the table and crouched there.

Pulling herself together, my aunt stood up and rolled up her sleeves.

"Get t'hell out a' me sight before I murder ya, Lily O'Shea, and don't *ever* come back here again!"

I never did, and I never got my acid drops or Mickey Mouse toffee either.

GOING FOR MAMMY'S MEDICINE

"Lily, will you please go over to Mercer Street Hospital and get my medicine. Take this bottle with you, love. The man'll know what I have by the label. It'll do me good, it's got iron in it. I'll feel better even after the first spoonful."

"Why's it always me that has to go? I hate goin' to that dispensary, an' it's so far!"

"An' listen, love," Mammy said, ignoring me, "on your way back I want you to call into Bewley's. Try an' see your Uncle Bob. Give him this note, to see if he'll loan me some money – an' he might give you a cake."

Whenever Mammy was worried or run down, she'd beg me to go to Mercer Street Hospital to get her medicine. She feared this hospital herself ever since she'd had her operation there.

"I'll never forget it," I heard her tell Mrs Murphy. "It was a dreadful experience. I woke up during the operation."

Mrs Murphy nodded, leaning against our door, her big red-blotched arms folded in front of her.

"God help ya, I'm not surprised. Sure dey're all students over dere in dat hospital, just like de dental. Mick haemorrhaged buckets for t'ree days after he had all his teeth out. Dey're all butchers."

Hearing this frightened the heart out of Mammy, and she never trusted dentists or doctors again. She had her own cures for us children: for a toothache, we held cold water in our mouths; for a cold in our insides, it was off to the pub with our Baby Power bottle for thrupence worth of peppermint. But, for herself, there was no other cure for her ailment except that iron tonic from Mercer Street Hospital dispensary.

Mercer Street Hospital was over the other side of the city. Carrying the empty medicine bottle, I ran all the way till I came to Grafton Street, then dawdled, gazing into the shop windows. It was so different here. There were no dealers selling their vegetables, fruit and fish outside these grand shops, and no papers or rubbish blowing around on the paths. Here in Grafton Street, porters in uniform held the doors open for ladies wearing fur coats and fox furs. But I was glad of the dealers in Parnell Street, especially when one of those old shawly women staggered out of a pub and bumped into me.

"The curse a' Christ on ya," she'd scream if she caught me glancing back at her.

The dealers' presence, rough and ready as they were, made me feel safe from these cranky old women.

The sound of Bing Crosby's voice drew me down a lane off Grafton Street to a little music shop. A gramophone with a large horn was playing in the window. An emblem of a proud dog in a sitting position was displayed on its shiny wood. His Master's Voice was written underneath. Inside the shop an old man was sorting out sheets of music. I hurried on, crossed over to the green and rushed up York Street towards Mercer Street Hospital. It was a huge grey stone building. As I looked down into the basement, gushes of water spurted out of the drain pipes and a strong smell of boiled cabbage sailed up to me. Hurrying by the front entrance, I came to the steps that led down to the hospital dispensary.

The dispensary was a small, cold, dreary room that stank of Jeyes Fluid. Shabbily dressed men and women sat tightly together on wooden benches in a semicircle, waiting their turns. Some were staring vacantly towards a narrow wooden shutter in the wall where the medicine was being dispensed. A card tacked to the wall above it warned, *Do Not Spit On Floor*.

The shutter was pulled across, and a small, thin man in a

white coat peered out. He beckoned with his finger to the next person in line to come forward to collect the medicine. The people moved slowly along the wooden benches without standing up. Some were coughing their hearts up into old bits of rag, while others dragged their crutches along. Men with caps on their laps crouched forward, put their heads in their hands and gazed glumly at the stone floor. Feeling squashed in between all these sick and cranky people, I'd stand up from time to time to straighten my dress under me. This greatly annoyed them.

"For Christ's sake, will ya tell that young wan to stay easy!" one of the women shouted.

They turned and glared at me.

The shutter slid across. It was my turn.

"Medicine for Missus O'Shea," I said, handing the man the empty bottle.

The shutter only stayed open long enough for me to get a quick glimpse of the rows and rows of shelves of large bottles full of different coloured liquids. After a few minutes he opened it and handed me a big bottle of browny-coloured mixture. A clean new white label, with scrawly handwriting, was stuck on the bottle, and a big brand new cork was pressed down on top.

Anxious to be away from the dispensary and the hospital, I hurried back towards Grafton Street to visit my Uncle Bob, who was the caretaker of Bewley's. I pushed open Bewley's door and peeped inside the shop to see if I could see him. The rich aroma of Bewley's coffee floated out to me. Well-dressed men sitting on cosy cushioned seats in secluded alcoves were reading their newspapers, drinking coffee and eating small iced cakes. I couldn't see my uncle anywhere and was too shy to go in. Uncle Bob lived in the caretaker's flat above Bewley's. The entrance was around the corner in Johnson Court. When I knocked hard on his door, a window above was pulled up and my Aunt Violy leaned out. She threw down a key wrapped up in a small piece of paper.

"Here's the key, Lily. Can you see yourself up?" she called down.

She gave me a note to take back to Mammy, but no money. I skipped back home with the medicine and told my pals that I had been to Grafton Street. And into Bewley's. And had a lovely pink iced cake. They looked at me in disbelief.

"Ya're not allowed in Bewley's, Lily O'Shea, so ya're not. Only the posh people can go in there."

"Well my uncle works there, and whenever he sees me, he gives me a cake, so he does."

Mammy read the note and said nothing, nothing at all.

JEM'S SHOP

Annie and I had just arrived home from school. The room was full of smoke, because Mammy had been burning our worn-out shoes to keep the fire in. Mr Campbell's bag of turf had run out, even though Mammy had dampened it.

"Listen, I hope youse don't mind, but would youse two mind going to that little shop at the top of Gardiner Street and getting me some turf."

"Not t'Jem's. I hate goin' there," I complained, staring at my old shoes curling up and shrivelling in the fire, the nails falling out like teeth.

"I tell youse what, if there's a ha'penny over youse can have it."

Jem's shop was down in the cellar of a rough tenement

house in Upper Gardiner Street. My sister and I hurried along pushing our old wobbly wheeled pram to carry the turf home in. Past the bus station on Mountjoy Square we went, and down Hutton's Lane with its row of tiny shabby white-washed cottages clustered close together. We stopped and stared sadly at the bunches of little rabbits, their fur and heads still on, hanging outside a butcher's shop in Parnell Street. Our heads were nice and warm with the pixie hoods that Mammy had made us out of old woollen scarves. Sleet was falling. Our hands were curled up inside the sleeves of our jerseys. My skirt hung well down below my coat. In the damp evening air my bare knees rubbed together making them red and sore.

As we neared Jem's shop, the tenements looked poorer and poorer. Faded flowery curtains were dragged across long dirty windows. The curtains were so skimpy they did not meet in the centre, and we could see the beds inside the rooms. The main hall doors were left wide open – all the time. Groups of men were smoking and swearing loudly as they gambled in the open halls, tossing pennies and ha'pennies. Big girls with messy uncombed hair stood on the steps out-side, holding their babies underneath their black shawls, act-ing like their mammies. We felt afraid passing these houses.

When we arrived at Jem's cellar, we leant up against the iron railings. With our feet stuck through the open bars, we peeped down the stone steps into the basement. We could barely see through its barred, dirty and dimly lit window. The strong fumes of paraffin, mixed with the sweet, damp earthy-bog smell of turf, drifted up to us.

Inside this dreary ice-cold shop, the turf was stacked up high in untidy piles on its stone floor. The flickering light of Jem's paraffin lamp threw shadows around the dirty walls. Several large drums of paraffin stood in a corner. The drums were fitted with small taps. Old bits of rags lay on the oil-stained floor beneath the taps to catch the drips. Groups of shabbily dressed men stood around, rubbing and blowing on their red chapped hands to keep warm. They were discussing the war. A couple of older women stood near by waiting patiently to be served paraffin to burn in their lamps. They were clutching their small empty tins. We looked at them, at their long black shawls hanging over their skirts and buttoned boots. Each one's grey hair was pulled back tightly in a bun. In the dim light, they stared back at us like two large crows.

"What's yer names? Where do youse live?"

"Fitzgibbon Street," we answered, moving back away from them.

Jem, in his old overcoat and fingerless gloves, looked over at us.

"What d'yas want?"

"Can we have a stone of turf, please?"

Jem slowly shovelled up the lumps of turf on to his large weighing scales that was balanced by a huge iron weight. He talked over our heads to his regular customers as he counted out our money into his tin box. We couldn't wait to see if there was a ha'penny change so we could buy broken Peggy-leg sweets displayed in large jars on a shelf behind him, next to his candles.

From the pile of old newspapers Jem had stacked on his counter, he tore a piece off, rolled it into a cone and dropped two lumps of Peggy-legs into it.

It was dark by the time we got out of the shop and the street lamps were lit. We dragged the pram, filled with turf, up the stone steps and hurried off home.

No Money for the Messages

It was great when Daddy was working on the roads in the Dublin Zoo. I'd bring up his lunch and get in for free. When he'd see me, he'd throw down his shovel and point towards the Lion House.

"Jaysus, Lily, will ya listen to those lions' roaring," he'd laugh. "They want to be fed. G'wan over and see 'em. The keeper will be shoving half a cow inta their cage."

But the Zoo job didn't last long, and Daddy was transferred back to the city, digging and tarring the roads again. He hated these jobs, but as he never went to school and could not read or write, this was the only work Mr Campbell could find him. I'd tremble every Friday night when I'd hear his footsteps trample loudly through the hall. I'd be worried sick that he'd be drunk and in one of his black moods again. A row would surely start when Mammy would ask him for money. He'd pick up his dinner and throw it into the fire, plate and all. Mammy's rabbit stew would hiss on the hot bars of the fire.

"I don't want that fuckin' slop!" he'd shout, his face twisted and ugly with anger. "You can tell yer fuckin' clergyman from me that he can keep his shaggin' job! See how he'd like it out there in the filth of the city diggin' the roads with a pick an' shovel."

Mammy would go white with fear when he'd grab up one side of the table to upend it.

Half crying, she would plead with him. "Please, John, don't! Don't!"

The sound of the delph smashing would send us all running out into the street screaming. Huddling close together next to the railings in front of our window, we'd still hear him swearing.

I wish Robbie was home, I'd think to myself, remembering

the last time there was a row. Robbie walked in just at the right moment, grabbed hold of Daddy and punched him up against the door. "Leave my mother alone," he screamed. But Robbie usually worked late in the laundry of a Friday night.

We would not go back inside our room till we saw Daddy leave. Mammy would be crying as she tried to clean up the place, lifting up chairs and gathering up broken delph.

Once Daddy, in one of his tempers, picked up our large glass fish ornament and smashed it into smithereens. It had stood on our mantelpiece, its wide-open mouth crammed full of buttons. Mr Campbell came to visit us soon after. Annie was sitting at our table singing our Sunday school hymn:

> Jesus loves me, this I know,
> 'Cause the Bible tells me so.

Mr Campbell and Mammy sat listening and smiling. Suddenly the words changed:

> Jesus, Jesus, me daddy broke the fish
> And all the buttons went over the floor.
> Dear, oh dear, what a terrible mesh.

"What is Annie singing?" Mr Campbell said smiling.

Annie sang it over again, this time louder. Mammy nearly died; she jumped up and pushed both of us towards to door.

"Will the two of youse, for God's sake, go outside and play," she snapped.

That evening, Mammy was standing talking to the other women at our hall door. I was standing in front of her, leaning against her, listening.

"My God," I heard her say, "I was so embarrassed when Annie sang about the broken fish in front of our clergyman."

The women roared with laughter as Mammy sang the hymn in Annie's words. But Mammy didn't tell them all her business. She didn't tell them about the evening when Daddy pushed her so hard that he sent her flying across the room, breaking her arm.

Things quietened down when Daddy threw down his spade with the Corporation and tried his hand at other ways of making money.

Bikes were a popular means of transport. Men who were lucky enough to have a good job relied on their bikes to get to work. They would bring their bikes to Daddy and pay him a small amount to mend their punctures.

After the bikes came the birds. I would hover around him as he gently wrapped each baby canary in cotton wool and lined them up on our kitchen chairs, so he could clean the cage.

Then there were the dogs. His friends would come to him with their mongrel dogs to dock their tails.

"Could you take a bit off its tail, John? Look at the length of it! I'll be back for him later," they'd say, running off.

I hated him doing this, and when I'd see him put the dog's tail on the stool and reach for the hatchet, I'd run like mad outside into the street. There'd be a loud yelp. A few minutes later, the dog would come running out after me, whining pitifully with a bandage on the remains of its tail.

Most of these jobs Daddy would do for little or nothing, so Mammy had to depend on Robbie's few bob every week.

No Penny for the Meter

The gas globe popped out. Our room was left dark and eerie. The light from the lamp-post outside our window streamed in, casting frightening shadows on our high ceiling.

"Mammy, can you put a penny in the meter?" I called out, looking up from an old comic that someone had loaned me.

"Jesus, I don't think I have one," Mammy said, shaking out her purse.

I sat there waiting in our armchair for her to find one.

"Look in Daddy's old overcoat, Mammy. D'ya 'member I found one there once down in the linin' amongst all the fluff."

Mammy sighed and began to clear the table in the near dark. She glanced up at the hungry gas meter hanging on the wall.

"Where's that scrap of wire I saw you fiddling with, Lily?" she said, slamming the cups and saucers back down on to the table.

"It's down in the grate. Here it is! What do you want it for?"

"Just come over here and hold that candle so I can see what I'm doing."

Mammy straightened the wire, stretched up towards the meter and gripped hold of the padlock. She poked the wire into the lock and wriggled it this way and that way. The main hall door banged. For a moment she stopped and listened. A man's heavy footsteps hurried through the hall, past our door and on up the stairs.

"Who's that I wonder?" she said quietly. "I don't know that footstep."

"Mammy, are ya nearly finished? Me arm is painin' me. Can I go outside?"

"Just wait a minute," she whispered, "I've nearly got it."

After what seemed like ages and ages, the padlock gave way and fell open. Mammy, shaking with fright, brushed her hair back and slipped off the lock. I watched as she pulled out the tray and took out the few pennies in there.

"I'll make it up. I'll put it back before the gasman comes again," she whispered.

The tray was quickly slid in with the padlock hooked on but left hanging open. One penny was pushed through its slot, and the rest went into her apron pocket.

"Now can I go out to play?"

"No, it's too late. Get the others in for bed," she said crossly.

A few weeks later, there was a sharp knock on our door.

"Gas! Gas!" a loud voice bellowed in the hall.

Mammy went into a panic.

"Jesus, Mary and Joseph. Where's that blasted lock? Who's been playing with it? I left it on the mantelpiece behind that dog."

The gasman was let in. He opened the padlock, pulled out the tray and shook out all that was in there. He was startled. There was nothing inside except a small lump of lead that had been melted and battered by Mammy with a hammer. She had repeatedly shoved it through the slot for a penny.

"Not another one," the gas man muttered, as he banged the tray back in and put a new lock on.

Mammy said nothing.

"Well, Missus," he said, his hand on our door, "I've had to cut yer gas off till ya pay yer bill!"

A JOB AT TRINITY

It was winter, 1940, and Mammy was finding it harder and harder to make ends meet. Every evening she'd rush down to the butcher's in Parnell Street when everything was cheaper and buy thrupence worth of lights – the insides of rabbits. With these hearts, livers and gizzards and a pennyworth of vegetables that the dealers had left over, she would make us a stew.

I loved cutting open the gizzards and cleaning the grit out.

But there were times when Mammy didn't even have these few pennies.

"I'll have to go and see Mr Campbell again," she'd sigh, pulling on her coat. And off she'd go.

"Don't worry," Mr Campbell would say, "here's two shillings to help you get by, and I'll talk to the gas people again about putting on your gas."

She didn't know herself when Mr Campbell came one day with the good news.

"Mrs O'Shea," he said, when she let him in, "I have a job for you in Trinity College. You are to replace a lady who is having a serious operation."

In her job in Trinity College, Mammy was to light the fires in the rooms where lectures were to be given that day. The fires had to be lit early in the morning and kept stacked up all day. During the lectures, she could sit and relax in a special room that was for her use only.

One morning Mammy said I could go and see her after school. It was icy cold and wet as I hurried along down O'Connell Street and over the bridge to Trinity College. A man standing inside its big iron gates stopped me from entering.

"Go around to the other gate."

I slipped inside a side gate, ran across a large yard and down the stone steps into Mammy's small room. The heat from the iron range hit me as soon as I entered.

"I can use as much coal as I like," Mammy told me happily, as she hung my wet coat and pixie hood in front of it.

Two cups and saucers, bread, butter, tea and sweet tinned milk stood on a tiny wooden table in front of a small barred window. A teapot was purring on top of the hot range. Mammy pulled open the door of the fire, bent down and held a thick piece of bread on a fork to toast for me. The jagged pieces of the bread crisped to a golden brown. She chatted away as she poured out my tea and buttered the toast. The toast didn't taste smoky like it often did at home. She could burn real coal here, not damp turf.

"This is a grand little job, Lily. It's a gift; it's a godsend. There's even a few bob over after I've got the messages. But it's not my job and I'll have to leave when that poor woman gets better," she reminded me and herself firmly.

"I suppose you wish you could keep it for ever?" I said smiling, sitting back in her comfortable chair, my feet stretched out towards the heat of the open range.

My fingers began to feel warm as they curled around my cup of sweet milky tea. I stared into the glowing red-hot coals dreaming.

I like being here with her on my very own. Mammy and I can talk about things together. And Daddy is in a good mood now that he can lie in bed all morning and go off on his own in the evenings. I hope Mammy can stay in this job. Maybe that woman who works here won't get better – perhaps she might even die!

"C'mon, Lily, hurry up! Put your shoes back on. It's time to go up to the lecture rooms to stack up the fires."

We went down to the cellar and filled up two buckets.

"Mind you don't knock any of the coal out on to the clean stairs," Mammy whispered to me as we carried the heavy buckets up to the rooms.

A professor on his way to class saw us struggling. He stopped and took one of the buckets from her and carried it on up the stairs to his room where she was to stack the fire.

"They are real gentlemen, Lily," Mammy said on our way home.

The professors looked like old men to me, especially the ones with the beards. They got to know Mammy and would often stop and talk to her about how she was coping. At night, we'd hear nothing else but what the professors had said during the day.

Unfortunately for Mammy, the woman did recover from her operation and was well enough to return to her job.

A RAT SLIPPED IN

Mammy constantly warned us to keep our door closed as we ran in and out of our room all day for a bit of bread and butter. She worried about the rats in our basement coming up and sneaking in. The rats carried dreadful diseases. They'd climb into people's beds in the night and bite them, particularly mothers with new babies. Then one day, when we forgot and left the door open, a rat, looking for food, slithered up from the basement, into the yard, through the dark hall, saw his chance and sneaked into our room.

"Jesus, Mary and Joseph, youse have gone an' let a rat in! Get up on the beds quick, all of youse!" Mammy screamed as she grabbed the sweeping brush.

She chased the rat around the room from corner to corner. Smutty, our big black tom-cat who was named after the smoky black smuts that blew out of our fire, scurried along beside her. Chairs were knocked over as she tried to belt the rat with the brush. We all shrieked in horror when the big grey rat turned, stood its ground and jumped up towards Mammy's throat. Smutty pounced on it. The rat fought back and bit him on the neck.

To our relief the door opened and Robbie, who was fifteen, walked in from work.

"Robbie! Robbie!" we shouted, jumping on the bed. "A rat's nearly bit Mammy, but Smutty's attacked him."

Mammy's face was flushed as she poked madly at the rat under our bed.

"It must have come up from the basement," she panted angrily.

"Gimme the brush," Robbie said, throwing his laundry coat on the bed.

We watched as he cornered the rat behind the wardrobe, beating it down every time it tried to attack. Finally, he picked up the dead rat by the tail and tossed it down into the area.

We looked at poor Smutty lying there badly bitten. He became ill, not wanting to go out. A big lump appeared on his neck. Mammy cut the fur around it, then made up a hot-bread poultice to draw out the infection, just like the poultice she put on Johnny's neck whenever he had an abscess.

Smutty lay there patiently every morning while Mammy tied a strip of old sheet over the poultice around his neck.

"He tried to save my life," she'd say, stroking him.

We made sure to bang the door behind us after that. When we moved to Cabra we left Smutty behind us in the tenements where he belonged.

SEASIDE EXCURSION TO KILLINEY

It was the day of our parish excursion. We were up early with our clean dresses on and our runners whitened. Mammy was in a fluster searching for something decent to wear.

"It's all right when you're at home," she sighed, "your apron covers everything."

"Hurry, Mammy, hurry, we'll be late for the train!"

"Go into the hall and wait for me till I get dressed."

"I wish she'd hurry," we said to each other as we jumped up and down on the stairs in the hall.

Mammy came hurrying out our door. It took her a good twenty minutes to get us all to Amiens Street Station.

"These shoes are crippling me," she kept saying, stopping to rub her feet. The shoes had been given to her by one of the ladies of our parish and were too small.

We were breathless as we struggled up the wide steps of Amiens Street Station. Mr Campbell and his wife were waiting on the platform.

"Good morning, Mrs O'Shea. Have you all got your tickets pinned on?" he said smiling.

As Mammy chatted to the other mothers, I wandered away from the group, staring at all that was going on around me. Slightly built porters dressed in heavy black jackets and peak caps grabbed up cases that people were struggling with. They stooped as they hurried towards the entrance trying to carry as many cases as they could.

"Get out a'me feckin' way," one said, bumping into me.

I gazed into the machine full of small bars of Cadbury's chocolate stacked up in neat rows and wondered how much money you needed to buy one. A man was thumping the side of a cigarette machine, cursing.

"I put me money in, but the feckin' Woodbines won't come out!"

A fortune teller machine caught my eye. It looked like a big silver weighing-scales. I climbed on, put my penny in and a small card dropped out. It read, "You will marry someone rich, have lots of children and live happily every after."

While I was lost in this dream, a train came puffing in with thundering bursts of thick black smoke. Its huge iron wheels, clanking on the tracks, screeched to a halt.

A short piercing whistle blew.

I turned around.

Mammy and our group were gone. A train was slowly chugging out of the station. I ran after it screaming. The stationmaster caught hold of my arm as I tried to pull open one of its doors. He bent down and read the card pinned on my dress: "St George's Parish, Church of Ireland. Excursion to Killiney."

"Ah God love ya, that was yer train all right."

Putting his arm around me, he took me over to a seat.

"Don't worry, love, I'll put ya on the next train to Killiney and I'll tell ya how many stations to count before it's time to get off. You'll see, yer Mammy will be waiting for ya at Killiney Station. Now, don't move from that seat," he called back, as he ran off to do his duties around the station.

I felt lonely and scared and lost interest in the excitement of the station. I thought about the great fun my sisters would be having on the excursion train. Mr Campbell would be going around the carriages handing out small bags of sweets and colourful streamers to all the children.

I'll get no sweets or streamers now, I sobbed to myself. I loved those streamers; they were like liquorice wheels, rolled up tightly into small whirls. *They'll all be leanin' out of their windows, lettin' them unwind. I'll miss the fun of tryin' to catch them as they flutter back from the carriage in front. Oh God.* I remembered last year when I was hanging out the window. The train went under a tunnel and a speck of ash blew back into my eye from the engine's smoke. My eye hurt and became watery. I rubbed and rubbed it, which only made it worse, leaving a black, sooty ring around my eye. Mammy laughed, but gave out to me for hanging out the window. She spat on her hanky and wiped my face.

An hour later, the stationmaster put me on the next train to Killiney. The train stopped at all the seaside resorts on the way. I made sure to count each station carefully. It seemed to take for ever all on my own in the carriage. Looking out of the window, I saw the remains of the colourful streamers caught on the tracks. At last the train pulled into Killiney. Mammy was standing on the platform staring with a worried face. She ran to meet me when she saw me jump off.

"Oh thank God, Lily, you're all right! In the name a' God, where were you? Why didn't you get on the train with all the other children?

Taking me by the hand, she rushed me down to the sea, all the while reassuring me that I hadn't missed anything.

The children were in the water, wearing their red and navy one-piece woollen bathing suits. Mothers were sitting in groups laughing and joking. The trauma of missing the train was forgotten.

The Protestant diocese owned a lot of property around the coastal resorts of Dublin. Our parish had access to a tearoom situated on a cliff overlooking the sea. In this tiny tearoom Mrs Campbell, with a couple of her friends from the parish, prepared lunch for us. They boiled water for our tea and made up delicious sandwiches of meat, cheese and jam. They were individually wrapped in small bags to keep out the sand.

Mr Campbell, standing up to organise us, looked hot under his straw boater hat.

"Sit in a circle and make a hole in the sand to hold your cup steady," he told us.

Looking up towards the tearoom on the cliff, we could see Mrs Campbell and the other ladies treading their way care-fully down narrow wooden steps, carrying large enamelled jugs full of sweet milky tea. As they bent down to pour the tea into our cups, their posh silk blouses had a nice soapy smell. We were all given a few sandwiches and a piece of fruit cake.

Mr Campbell, his wife and the other ladies sat together.

During the afternoon Mr Campbell, still in his full clerical clothes, planned games for us children. A group of four children would race a short distance along the damp sand for a small bag of sweets. He made sure we all won a race. There was also a special prize for the winner who built the best sand castle. Mammy sat back, relaxed and forgot her worries.

At the end of the day, a piece of fruit was passed around to each of us. Tricking around with each other, we headed back up to Killiney Station.

"Jesus!" we laughed, jumping well back to avoid the scalding steam that hissed out of the train's huge engine.

On the train home we were tired and quiet, thinking about all the fun we'd had during the day. Back in the city, we said our goodbyes.

Paper boys ran around the station shouting out the latest news on the bombing of London. Dawdling home, we walked around groups of rowdy men standing at corners outside pubs.

"Mammy, what are they arguing about?" we asked, looking back at them.

"Ah, it's about England and the war. Come on! Don't worry, we're neutral. We'll never be bombed!"

NORTH STRAND BOMBING

The Second World War began for me on the night of 31 May 1941. Two German bombers dropped bombs by mistake on Dublin's North Strand area, killing thirty-four people. They claimed they were dumping bombs on their way home, apologised for it twenty years later and paid compensation.

It was Saturday night. We were awakened by the sound of a loud explosion. Our tenement house shook, the window rattled and the plates slipped down off our dresser.

"Jesus, Dublin's being bombed!" Mammy cried as she frantically dragged our beds away from the window. "Robbie, can you pull those shutters across the window?"

One by one, we could hear our neighbours rushing down the stairs. Mammy hurried out into the hall to speak to them. Lying in bed bewildered, we could hear Mr Murphy.

"Oh it's a bomb all right. Jesus Christ, aren't we supposed to be neutral?"

Mammy stayed up all night, running in and out of our room, her coat around her shoulders, urging us to try and go back to sleep.

Word soon got around that the North Strand had been bombed. Next morning after mass, women huddled around their doorways worried sick that Dublin was now going to be bombed every night like London. Each one, including Mammy, had a story to tell about a friend or relative living in England. I liked Mammy's story the best.

"Listen till I tell ya," I heard her say as she moved closer to the women. "My sister in England has been bombed twice, just imagine, twice! God help her. Each time she came out of the shelter with her children, her house would be gone. No wonder her nerves got the better of her and she sometimes walks backwards."

This walking backwards really intrigued me. Whenever I heard this story, I'd walk backwards, trying to understand what it was like.

A few days after the bombing, I went down to the North Strand with the other children of our street. We were relieved to see the Strand Cinema still standing where we had just seen Bud Abbott and Lou Costello in *Hold that Ghost*. A row of houses and a small Church of Ireland church had been demolished. We rummaged through the church's rubble. Mammy was shocked when I brought home a pile of half-burnt hymn books.

Ireland was under pressure at this time from England to participate in the war, or at least allow the British to use Irish ports as naval bases. The prime minister, de Valera, refused because Ireland, with an ill-equipped army, was undefended and unprepared, with no air raid shelters or gas masks for the people.

After the North Strand bombing, I became aware of ugly concrete air raid shelters around the streets. Gas masks were being issued. We felt excited going to be fitted for one, but the gas masks in their nice new boxes were taken from us and stacked under the beds with everything else.

"They're not for playing with," Mammy warned us.

Coal became scarce and neighbours complained bitterly as they wheeled their prams loaded with turf into the hall.

"Isn't the coal gone very dear, Missus?" they called out to Mammy, who was standing talking to Mr Murphy.

As usual, Mr Murphy knew all the answers. He'd heard it all in the pub.

"It's 'cause England's cut back on our coal, that's why. She's not lettin' her coal boats come into our ports. Ah well, God's good, and we'll just have t'make do with our turf," he said, heading up stairs.

Bread and butter were the main food for most large families. When these became rationed, it made life hard for mothers trying to make do with their weekly supply. Nothing comforted a small child more than a piece of bread and butter with sugar sprinkled on it.

A mixture of cod-liver oil and Parish's Food was spooned into us every night. Mammy would shake the bottle well to stir up the brown, watery Parish's Food that settled at the bottom.

"Swallow it! You need it to keep you healthy," Mammy would shout at me when I'd heave and nearly vomit.

And I hated having to stand in a queue every Friday for hours outside Beckett's of Earl Street to receive our small ration of tea. Tea was the cure for everything. It soothed the nerves of worried mothers, fretful babies had their bottles filled with it and it was even used for sore eyes.

"Tell your mammy to bathe your eyes in cold tea," Mammy would tell Mary, when she'd call for me.

Mary always had styes in her eyes.

Tea leaves were never thrown out. They'd be used over and over again. Those who could afford it bought tea on the black market for three times the normal price.

The cutting off of wheat imports from England meant the end of white bread. The bread became a dirty-brown colour and was blamed for causing scabies.

In bed at night, when the shutters were drawn and the gas light turned down, we'd often hear the low drone of planes.

"I hope they're not the Germans going over to bomb Belfast," Mammy would whisper, poking the fire. "Say a prayer for the poor people living there."

It puzzled me when she'd ask us to say a prayer for Granny Crawte as well. Were people not even safe in heaven? When Daddy was out, I'd add a prayer for him.

Please, God, don't let him come home again. It's more peaceful without him.

Mammy was delighted when he found work on the Irish boats as a fireman.

"At last, we might get on our feet," she'd say happily. But it didn't work out like that.

After weeks of being away on a trip, he'd come home drunk with little or no money. But hidden in the lining of his coat would be a delicious fresh white pan loaf, which was a luxury.

"I swear t'God, Doll," he'd reassure Mammy, looking up to heaven, "the skipper gave it t'me from the galley."

Other times, he'd have a large tin of malt, which tasted like toffee, or a huge tin of strawberry jam with whole strawberries.

It was not long before Dublin became complacent again. The air raid shelters became filthy places. The dark, damp walls stank of urine; even lovers didn't go in them any more. The shelters were now homes for rats, drunkards and strange characters.

"Don't go in there, love, it's smelly and dirty," mothers would call down from tenement windows.

Children began to play in the street with their gas masks. Mammy turned a blind eye when we climbed under our bed and dragged out ours. Young fellas ran around the streets with them on playing war games, shouting to each other through the smelly rubber. It was just as well Dublin was never bombed again.

MR MURPHY GOES AND DIES

"Mammy, why do we have to have the curtains pulled over and we can't even look out?"

"Out of respect for Mister Murphy," Mammy said patiently, "and they'll stay pulled till he's buried."

"Everyone seems to be dyin' lately," I complained. "Even Mister Murphy goes and dies!"

Daddy was standing in front of our small mirror trying to shave. A basin of water stood on a chair beside him. He was in a good mood, whistling away. He had a few days' leave from the boats and was going out.

"Why can't they go out to play?" he said as he rinsed his razor in the water.

"John, Mister Murphy is going to the chapel. The undertaker is up there now, and I don't want them running in an' out of the hall getting under the men's feet."

Mammy went over to the door and put her ear up against it.

"For God's sake, please be quiet just for a minute! I think the coffin is being carried down now."

A morbid silence fell over the house. All we could hear was the shuffle of men's heavy footsteps on the wooden stairs as they struggled down the few flights with the coffin. Holding myself, I pleaded to be let go outside to the lavatory.

"Come straight back," Mammy whispered, opening the door quietly and glancing up the stairs towards Murphys'.

Our hall door was pushed wide to the back. A breeze blew into the hall. A few women stood outside in the street looking in curiously.

"Steady lads, easy now," the undertaker said as they carried Murphy around the last narrow landing.

Frightened of seeing Mr Murphy's coffin, I didn't want to go any more and quickly slipped back into our room.

"Well, that's the end a' poor awl Murphy," Daddy said, dabbing his face with an old towel on the back of a chair. "I'll tall ya what though, he was fond a' the drink, was awl Murphy. And I suppose they'll be all stopping off at the Brian Boru on their way back from the funeral to give him a good send off."

"Yes, but all the same, John, he never left Missus Murphy short. And d'ya know what? She washed him and shaved him herself. She wouldn't let anyone else touch him."

On the day of the funeral, the hearse drove past our

window three times before heading for Glasnevin Cemetery. Mrs Murphy was wearing her old coat dyed black.

"D'insurance money wasn't enough t'buy a new one," she told Mammy. "An' it was either ha' me awl coat dyed black or sew a star on me sleeve."

"Who's carrying the coffin?" Mammy asked, knowing Murphy's sons weren't big enough.

"Ah, his brothers will. Sure dat's how he'd want it, Lord ha' mercy on him!"

YOU'RE AWFUL, MAMMY, YOU'RE AWFUL

"Mammy, can you give me some money for chips? Everybody's buying some. Everybody is!" I pleaded with my mother, following her around our room.

It was a cool autumn evening and I had just come in from playing in the street. Mammy looked worn out. She went over to the sunken fire, poked it angrily and then threw a bucket of cinders over it to keep it going.

"I haven't got a penny for the meter, never mind chips," she shouted at me.

"I wish Granny hadn't died," I whinged, stamping into her little room.

It was in between lights, neither day nor night, and Granny's room looked dreary. I was drawn towards her fire that was lighting. Mammy had put our big black iron pot on it, and it was bubbling away. I sat down on the stool in front of the fire and shoved my foot up on the hob where Granny's teapot normally rested. My foot slipped, hit the pot and knocked it over. The fire hissed as the scalding hot water poured out and splashed all over my feet. Hearing me scream, Mammy rushed in.

"Jesus, Mary and Joseph, Lily! What have you done? What have you done?"

She grabbed my feet up against her apron and pulled my sandals and socks off. We both stared in horror.

"Mammy, me skin's come off in me socks," I sobbed, looking at my red raw feet.

Shaking with fright, she tried to calm me.

"You'll be all right, love, you'll be all right. Wait there, I'll be back in a minute."

She hurried upstairs to Mrs Murphy and borrowed her old pram. I was lifted into it. With my knees bent up in the pram, Mammy ran with me to the children's hospital in Temple Street, which was about fifteen minutes away.

In the 1940s the poor had no alternative but to get their injured children to hospital themselves. The only time we saw an ambulance was when a child was dying of scarlet fever, diphtheria or one of the other dreadful diseases that were around then. Seeing the ambulance coming up our street, all the women would stop talking and look in fear, some blessing themselves – especially when the ambulance pulled up outside their tenement house. The driver would jump out holding a red woollen blanket, which was a sure sign it was from Jervis Street Hospital. He'd rush into the tenement, straight to the very room he wanted, and within minutes would be out again carrying a child wrapped up in the blanket.

While we were waiting in the long queue at the hospital, a mother rushed in with her baby who was having a fit. The woman looked at us.

"I had her in hospital, Missus. She was a forceps, that's what happened to her. She was a forceps."

"God love her," Mammy nodded.

I knew about fits. I'd often seen children take them in the street. *But what is this about forceps?* I wondered. *T'ank God I'm not goin' into hospital.*

When my feet were finally bandaged, Mammy was told to bring me back every day to have them dressed. So every morning after she got my brother and sisters off to school, she would wheel me in the pram to the hospital for a clean dressing. I was ten years old and felt very embarrassed sitting in this baby's pram. Mammy wheeled me to and from the hospital for a whole week, but my feet got worse.

"This child's feet have gone septic. She must be admitted," the doctor said in his cold, clinical tone.

Penicillin was not available at that time, and it was not unusual to see people around the city with limbs missing, lumps on their necks and disfigurements.

Mammy looked terribly worried: she didn't trust them. Before I knew what was happening, a big country nurse lifted me up to take me to a ward. Parents were not permitted to see their children settled in.

"You're awful, Mammy, you're awful!" I screamed, reaching out for her.

How I'd dread to see the doctor coming around with the nurse every morning. He'd take hold of a corner of the dressing and whip it off, leaving my feet bleeding. So in the early hours of the morning, I'd bend down under the wire cage that held the covers off my feet and, bit by bit, slowly remove the tightly stuck dressing before the doctor arrived.

I had my eleventh birthday in hospital, and my school teacher, Mrs Bradshaw, came to visit me. She brought me a *Film Fun* annual and a box of cakes. This was a great treat and a surprise as Mrs Bradshaw rarely spoke to you outside the classroom. She sat on a chair close to me, and I could smell her nice face powder. I was shy, not sure of what to say to her.

It was strange to see her, this well-dressed lady sitting next to me talking in her posh accent, out of the classroom.

The nurses were kind and would tie a big bow of ribbon in my short brown hair every day. I was in a ward with babies and, as soon as I was allowed up, they gave me the job of giving the babies their bottles.

When it was time to leave the hospital, Mr Campbell arranged for me to go to a convalescent home in Stillorgan. This Protestant home was for men and women recovering from operations and serious illnesses. I loved it here as they made such a fuss of me, and I made friends with a boy of my own age. We'd chase each other across fields, picking and eating the blackberries galore. Being city children, we enjoyed the freedom of the countryside.

Mammy came to take me home a few weeks later.

"Look, Lily!" she said. "Look what I've got for you, a lovely new coat with a hat to match. It was your cousin's. I bought it off your Aunt Violy."

When the bus dropped us off in the city, we hurried up Parnell Street towards Mountjoy Square and home. I felt grown up in my new red and grey check coat with the matching hat trimmed with red velvet. I was happy that I would not have to wear my brother's laundry coat any more. When we arrived at our house, neighbours were standing outside our hall door. They stopped talking when they saw me.

"Ya're a terrible young wan, Lily O'Shea," they said, grabbing hold of my arm. "D'ya know yer poor Mammy cried all the way home from hospital, wheelin' that empty pram, after ya at t'been screamin' after her. Ya're a terrible young wan!"

Mammy smiled.

"Come on, love, I'll buy you those chips."

But I wasn't interested. I had spotted Sonny Boy Smith. I left Mammy and ran across the street to tell him my experiences.

THE OTHER WOMAN

When Daddy had spells of not working on the boats, he'd drag himself out of bed halfway through the day. Without even looking at any of us, he'd pace up and down, up and down, like the lions and tigers in their cages in Dublin's Zoo. Occasionally, he'd stop and gaze out our window at people going by in the street. As Daddy could not read, he only knew what Mammy read out to him or what he heard in the street. The only time he picked up a paper was when the fire wouldn't start. He'd hold it up close to the fire to create a draft, then leave it there till the paper turned brown and burst into flames.

Suddenly his dark mood would lift.

"I'm goin' out!" he'd say to himself out loud.

Feeling his chin, he'd bend and peer into a small mirror hanging on the wall. Sitting on the edge of my bed, I'd watch him. He'd swing around, and before I could escape, he'd grab me and rub his coarse bristly chin against my face. I'd squeal and push him away.

"Here, love, get me a Woodbine and blade," he'd say, handing me two pennies.

I'd run next door to Flynn's. Flynn's sold everything, not only fruit cake, butter and cheese, but also hairnets, pins, laces, small bundles of sticks, cigarettes and razor blades.

"A Mac's Smile blade, please, and a Woodbine," I'd say to Miss Flynn shyly.

Single blades and cigarettes were kept in two small flat boxes behind her. On my way back, I'd gaze at the blade. On one side of its wrapper, there was a picture of an unshaven man with a round grumpy face, and when you turned it upside down, the man's face became clean shaven and happy. Mac's Smile was written underneath.

I'd enjoy watching Daddy shaving. Pouncing on me, he'd dab a soapy shaving brush on my nose. He'd whistle happily as he dressed to go out. With great care, he'd cut out a piece of thick cardboard to cover the huge hole in his shoe, then tuck it inside. Holding up one of his shoes in his hands, he'd spit on it and polish it vigorously with an old rag until it shone. Looking down at himself proudly, he'd tighten his leather belt and brush his trousers down well with his hands. He'd snatch his overcoat off his bed and shake it. Then, rubbing a small lump of butter in the palms of his hands, he'd smooth his hair back and call out a cheery goodbye to Mammy.

"Mammy, where's Daddy gone off to?" I'd ask as he'd close the door behind him.

"T'God only knows where!" she'd whisper to herself, wringing out the floor cloth angrily into a bucket of dirty water. Straightening up, she'd dry her hands in her apron and pin up the loose strands of her long black hair that had come undone.

Daddy looked handsome and smart hurrying out towards the street. Mammy would rush to the window and stare after him. She wasn't the only one: the women standing around our hall door would move back to let him pass, then nod to each other.

"Where's O'Shea off to again, I wonder, all dressed up?" I'd hear them mutter as I skipped out to play.

One evening, just after Daddy had left, Mammy banged off our window and beckoned to Kathleen and me to come in from playing in the street.

"Quick!" she said. "Follow your father and see where he has been going to every night. Don't let him see you, for God's sake! Then hurry back and tell me."

I was reluctant to go and felt nervous, yet excited, as if I were playing a game. Kathleen, keen to go and needing no encouragement, persuaded me to go along with her. It was dusk when we started to hurry after him towards an area of private houses where our posh parishioners lived. At times, he'd glance back and we'd quickly duck behind a lamp-post. Children didn't play outside with each other in these streets as we did in the tenements. It was quiet, and the long dark shadows from the street lamps made me feel lonely and afraid. We lost sight of him.

"Let's go home," I said to my sister, but she insisted we continue and urged me to run with her.

We caught up with Daddy just in time to see a woman join him. She had been standing against a railings in the shadows. He tucked her arm in his with familiarity and they strolled away talking intimately. She was well dressed in a smart coat with a fur collar and a fashionable hat.

"Let's go up to him and give him a fright," Kathleen said.

"Hello, Daddy," we said, looking up at him and glaring at her.

He looked shocked. Dropping the other woman's arm, he put his hand in his trousers pocket and gave us thrupence each.

"Don't tell yer Mammy, will youse not!" he begged us.

We never answered him, but turned back in the direction of our home. Clutching the thrupenny piece tightly in my hand, I ran home as fast as I could to tell Mammy.

We went to bed quietly that night, dreading Daddy coming home. Mammy came and tucked us in, her lips tight. Annie looked at her and became anxious.

"Please, Mammy," she begged, "don't say anyt'in' to Daddy about that woman, sure ya won't?"

"Go to sleep, it'll be all right," Mammy whispered.

But it wasn't all right. The following morning, Annie and I were playing with the tap out in the backyard when we heard shouting and swearing and the sound of delph smashing coming from our room. It was Daddy. Mammy was crying and pleading with him to stop. Without turning the tap off, Annie and I ran through the hall screaming out into the safety of the street.

PART 2:
CABRA, BENBURB STREET
AND CABRA WEST

WE MOVE TO CABRA

"**B**eep-beep, beep-beep," blew Lord Mayor Alfie Byrne's horn as he rode up Fitzgibbon Street on his little motor scooter, waving to everyone. He was a small, elegantly dressed man, popular with the tenement women. Hanging out of tenement windows, they would shout down to him.

"I'm comin' down, Alfie; I want to talk to ya."

"Alfie," one would plead, putting her hand on his arm, "can you put in a good word for me in the Corporation offices for a house?"

Alfie would take out his notebook and pen and promise to do all he possibly could.

"God bless you, Alfie," she'd call after him as he rode away, tipping his top hat and beeping his horn.

It was the dream of most tenement mothers to be given a small Corporation house out of the city. These little pebble-dash houses were being built on the north and south side of Dublin to relocate the large families living in tenement rooms. The demand was great, and unless someone put a good word in for you, you could be waiting for years. Mothers with babies in their arms persecuted the men behind the counter in the Corporation offices in Lord Edward Street, although some wouldn't take the house that was allotted to them; they'd be wanting a house of their own choice. Mammy and I could be there for hours, upstairs in the narrow, stuffy offices behind crowds. Most were like Mammy and Mrs Murphy: they just wanted a house.

One morning, the Corporation gave Mammy a key to a new house in Cabra. A few days later the Murphys got one in Crumlin. We were so caught up in the excitement of moving that Mary and I didn't stop to think that we wouldn't see each other again.

When the day came for us to move, my father was away at sea on one of his trips. Mammy sent us all out to play while she tied up our clothes in bundles.

"Now stay outside," she warned us. "I don't want youse in here getting under the man's feet. Come in when he's gone!"

Before leaving the tenement, I ran outside into the yard and fetched my piggy-tin from the cistern over the lavatory. Then we rushed up towards Phibsborough and our new house in St Eithne Road, Cabra.

"There it is: number 11," Kathleen shouted. "It's a corner house."

We ran through the empty house, deeply inhaling the smell of newly painted windows and walls. I lay down on the floorboards and rubbed my hands along the fresh, clean, creamy wood, feeling its smoothness. Johnny flicked a switch and a light went on. It was magic. We all had a go.

A room with a small fireplace looked out into the front garden and street. Though it was the main room, it was called the kitchen. A tiny scullery, with a black iron stove, led off this room. A deep stone sink hung under a window.

"Oh, that's a grand sink to wash the clothes in," Mammy said, touching it, delighted with herself. "An' I won't have to go outside to wash the cabbage either."

"An' look, Mammy, here's a bath!" I said, opening a door next to the sink. "We won't need our old tin bath."

A lavatory was just outside the back door.

"This is our lavatory," Sylvia said, staring in at it. "No one else can use it. Isn't that right, Mammy?"

"C'mon upstairs," Annie's voice echoed down to us. "There's two lovely bedrooms."

A horse and cart pulled up outside our house. We recognised our belongings piled high on the open cart: our brass and iron bed ends, the wire bed springs, fibre mattresses, clothes tied up in bundles and, right on top, our one big old armchair.

Getting On Our Feet

There were no fences between the front gardens in Corporation houses, only a single iron railing. The back garden had even less – a mere strip of wire separated you from your neighbour. Soon sheets of rusty corrugated iron and old beds ends appeared all around back gardens as makeshift fences.

Our back garden was so big we couldn't manage it, so after turning over the big sods of black peaty soil, I got an idea.

"Let's pile it all up in the middle, Mammy," I said, "an' then we don't have to worry about the other end of the garden. We'll just have a little garden."

Annie and I took turns cutting the grass in our front garden with our big scissors, the ones that my father brought home from the boats.

"I wish we had shears like Daltons," we moaned, looking at the blisters on our fingers.

Mr Dalton was our neighbour. He had a garden of flowers. Not long after we moved in, he complained about our overgrown garden.

"Your grass and weeds are spreading into my garden," he said in his broad country accent.

This upset Mammy. She told Robbie all about it that evening.

"T'hell wit' dat awl bugger an' his garden," Robbie said, getting up from the table.

People settled in well and had pride in their new homes. They kept their windows sparkling and tried to outdo each other with fancy lace curtains and shiny brass letter boxes. Our windows had bright flowered cotton curtains. Mammy had made these by hand and hung them up with a wire.

Then Mammy saw a fender she wanted. She scrimped and scraped to save the five shillings to pay for it.

"Lily, you'll have to help me carry it home," she said one Saturday morning. "It's in a second-hand shop near St Peter's Church. The man said he'd deliver it by horse and cart if I gave him another shilling, but I can't afford it."

As we hurried down Connaught Street towards Phibsborough, Mammy bent down and picked up a bit of coal.

That's for luck!" she said, spitting on it. Mammy would never pass the tiniest bit of coal in the street.

We crossed Cabra Road, into the shop, and handed the man the five shillings.

"Isn't it lovely, Lily? It's a real bargain."

We both stood staring at the fender with its intricate iron lacework.

"C'mon, you have to help me," Mammy said, quickly bending down and lifting up one end.

"Oh God, Mammy, it's awful heavy!" I said, dropping it.

"Look, Lily, take a good grip underneath it with both hands."

I pulled the sleeves of my jersey down over my hands and lifted it. Mammy chatted as we struggled along, her back to me, leading the way.

"It'll go great in front of the fire, look real homely."

The soft, hazy rain didn't matter, nothing could dampen Mammy's spirits now that she was on her way home with this fender. As we walked slowly past grand private houses, I wondered to myself whether it had once belonged in one of them.

140

"Where d'you t'ink the man got the fender from, Mammy?"

"Oh, someone probably ran into debt and had to break up their home. It's easier to break a home than make one."

Just then I spotted a group of boys from our street coming in our direction. Without a word, I dropped my end of the fender and ran down Dalymount Lane to hide. I was ashamed of the boys' seeing me carrying this fender with Mammy. When the boys passed, I ran back and helped her carry it the rest of the way home.

This iron fender took pride of place in our home. It looked huge in front of our small fireplace. Mammy black-leaded and polished it every Saturday without fail. Our armchair sat next to it, and two wooden kitchen chairs were placed near by.

The fender welcomed us towards the fire. On long, cold winter evenings when the coalman had just been, we'd sit around our fire, our feet up on the fender. The fire would be backed up with glowing red-hot cinders. We'd chat about our teachers and all the news we'd heard from other children in school and on the streets. We'd all want to poke the fire as we talked. This caused arguments amongst us. Sometimes we'd wrap a piece of silver paper around the hot poker to curl our hair, which would often singe, frizzle and burn. Mammy would lose her patience, grab the poker off us and send us up to bed.

But Mammy didn't always get bargains. Now and again she was swindled, like the time a man sold her a cupboard. It was late at night and I had just come in from playing in the street. Our hall door was open.

"What's that handcart doin' outside our gate, Mammy?" I called out.

"I'm buying a cupboard to put your clothes in," she whispered, pointing to a man struggling upstairs with something.

"Ya're very lucky. Only a shillin' a week," the man said, hurrying back down.

The small, thin-faced man in the greasy dustcoat went off with his handcart and Mammy's shilling.

"I'm really getting on my feet. I've got the fender; now I'm buying a cupboard."

At last we had something to put our clothes in.

Not long after, I noticed small piles of sawdust on the floorboards near the cupboard.

"Mammy, what's that on the floor?"

My mother dragged out the cupboard and examined it.

"Oh my God, it's riddled with woodworm. I've been swindled. I'm wasting poor Robbie's hard-earned money. God, what would he think?"

Mammy was no good at arguing with the swindlers of Dublin. She tried to give it back to him the first Friday he came for his money.

"The cupboard you sold me is full of woodworm," she said crossly.

"Sure what's a bit a' woodworm, Missus! It's still a good cupboard," he said, holding out his hand, his foot in our door.

Every Friday night for the next five weeks, the thin-faced man in the greasy dustcoat knocked on our door for his money.

"Mammy, it's Swindler! It's Swindler!" I'd shout out, forgetting who I was talking to.

Swindler would stand there at the open door, not a bit bothered, as if Swindler were his real name! He'd wait till Mammy dried her hands and searched around for a shilling.

DOWN TO THE DOCKS FOR MONEY

We only saw my father every couple of months, usually the evening after his boat had docked. I'd be outside our gate playing with my pals, a taxi would pull up, and he'd fall out drink.

"Hello, love!" he'd shout over. "Are ya not goin' t'give yer daddy a big kiss?"

Ashamed of my life, I'd turn away. He'd stagger off towards our door singing:

Oh Maggie Maggie May,
They've taken you away,
Away across the Irish Sea.
You've robbed so many sailors,
The skippers off the whalers,
You'll never rob another any more.

Next morning, he'd promise Mammy faithfully that he'd leave her a weekly allowance while he was away at sea.

"I swear t'God, Doll, the money will be there for ya. Just wait a week," he'd say, spitting on his shoes as he polished them.

"You will now, John, won't you! I'm not even getting anything from Robbie."

Robbie had joined the Royal Navy and had to train in Gravesend Sea School for six months before he got paid.

Mammy would plead with me to go down to the shipping offices on the quays to get her allowance.

"It should be there now," she'd say, "and when you come home, love, I'll give you something for yourself."

Her absolute faith in my father convinced me that the money would be there, and I'd skip off happily for the bus. Women would be in the shipping office collecting their allowances when I'd arrive. They knew each other and chatted together. While waiting my turn to be served, I'd walk around this small office looking at the wonderful paintings of ships on the walls. The *City of Antwerp* was my favourite. The well-dressed man behind the counter would finally call me over and go down a list with me in a big black, hard-covered book.

"Hm ... John O'Shea. John O'Shea," he'd mutter to himself, slowly searching for my father's name.

Then he'd turn the book around towards me, so I could see the names as well. I'd recognise the names of the other men on the list who were working on the same ship as my father. They were all leaving their wives an allowance.

"I'm so sorry, but your father's name is not on the list," he'd say sympathetically. "He still hasn't signed the form like the other men have."

Tears would sting my eyes with disappointment and anger. I'd come home tired and upset.

Once when Mammy became desperate for money, she begged me to go down to the North Wall when Daddy's boat was due to arrive back in Dublin.

"Please, Lily, go and, for God's sake, try and get something out of him. Catch him before he has time to leave the boat. I'd go myself, but I've got nothing decent to wear."

I looked at her. She was wearing an old worn-out cardigan that was far too big for her, and the zip in her skirt was broken, bulging open. Her shoes were old with heels worn down on one side. Her large dark eyes pleaded with me to go.

"Besides, Lily," she said, "he'll give it to you before he'd give it to me, and he'd only try to drag me off to drink with his friends in the pub."

I thought of the times she had gone to meet him. She would arrive home late, alone, upset and with very little money. Waiting for her to come home, we would worry that something had happened to her and we'd be left all on our own.

I put my best coat on, the one Mammy bought me when I came out of hospital. I was growing out of it and my brown skirt hung well down below it. I had to get two buses, one into the city and one down to the docks. Sitting in the bus, I wished that I didn't have to go to get the money.

I thought of the Murphys. Mrs Murphy had never had to send her children to the docks for money. I had often heard her tell Mammy that when Murphy was paid off after a trip, he would never open his pay packet. He pinned his packet to his vest inside his shirt and borrowed money for drink. Many is the time I had seen him being dragged up the stairs, his two friends holding him up between them. I would follow behind and watch curiously as Mr Murphy's limp feet click-clacked on each stair. The men would quickly leave. Before the door closed, Mrs Murphy would roll him over, unbutton his shirt and, without fail, there would be his pay packet pinned to his vest, unopened.

Finally the bus arrived in O'Connell Street. I hurried for the next bus, which dropped me close to the docks. I felt afraid and lonely as I stumbled along on the cobblestone road. There were no paths. Now and again, an open-back lorry rumbled by to or from the boat. Men were passing cargo from the boat to other men loading up their lorries. They stopped working and whistled.

"Who are ya looking for, love?" they called over, smiling at me.

"John O'Shea, my father! Has he signed off yet?"

"I'm afraid he has," one replied. "All the men have been paid off a couple of hours ago. He might be in the local where they all drink. If not, he could be in Mulholland's."

"T'anks," I said, half crying, and started to run in the direction they pointed.

145

I was anxious to be away from the men as they nodded to each other knowingly. I ran past rows of small terraced houses.

I've got a good chance of findin' him, I told myself. By now he'd have a few drinks in him and he'd be feeling merry. He'd act the good kind father in front of his friends.

Oh God, it's gettin' dark. The lights are goin' on. I wish Mammy hadn't sent me. I hate him. Oh God, those boys standin' at the corner are watchin' me. They look rough and common. Please God, don't let them chase me. They might corner me and push me up against that wall. I'll run faster and I'll t'ink of somet'in' happy – what I'll do with the shillin' Mammy has promised me. I know, I'll go to the pictures tomorrow and buy some sweets. Oh t'ank God, here's the pub. I hope he's in here and hasn't got too drunk.

On entering the pub, I was immediately aware of men's loud voices as they stood around the bar, talking and arguing, drinking huge glasses of Guinness. Most of them were seamen with bundles at their feet. As I felt the barman watching me, my heart thumped with fright. I knew that children were not allowed inside a pub on their own, and any minute now he might order me out. My eyes searched through a thick smoky haze where men and women were sitting around tables on comfortable chairs. *If he is in here,* I told myself, *it's at one of these tables he'll be.* Sure enough, there he was sitting with all his friends and their wives, laughing and joking – the life and soul of the party. The women did not look like Mammy: they wore bright-coloured blouses with large gold-tinted buttons; their faces were heavily made up with lipstick, powder and rouge; they talked loudly and drank heavily with their husbands.

"Hello, Daddy," I smiled, tipping him softly on the shoulder.

He half rose from his chair with a look of surprise and delight on his face.

"Ah God, love, hello. Are ya all on yer own? Ah God, she's

all on her own," he said turning to his friends. "This is my little girl, everyone. She's come all the way down here just to see me. She's the only one that looks like me, the others are all the image of their mammy."

He looked up at me.

"See that chair over there, love, drag it over here beside me and I'll buy you a lemonade, and tell me, how's yer mammy?"

He knew why I had really come. After a few minutes, he reached into his trousers' pocket and pulled out a handful of notes.

"You see, love," he said loudly, so his friends could hear, "I had this money put by for yer mammy, and I'll give it to her meself when I get home."

I had lost trust in him. I knew that if I didn't get the money from him now, he would drink it all, so I sat there sipping the lemonade begging him.

"Daddy, can you give me the money to take home? Mammy needs it to get the messages."

The women at the table had gone silent. They were listening intently with big friendly smiles on their faces. Daddy was watching them. He tried to laugh it off.

"Will ya listen to her, for Jaysus sake? She doesn't believe me."

His voice warned me that he was becoming impatient, but his blue eyes were still smiling.

One of the women leaned over the table and gently touched my plaits.

"She's a lovely girl, John, God bless her. An' God love her all the same, she's come all the way down here to get some money for her mammy."

Daddy looked over at the men sitting at the table for support, but they sat back and avoided looking at him. They quietly gulped down their pints of Guinness. He took out a bundle of notes and handed it to me, then lifted his glass and emptied it. The foam from the head of the Guinness remained above his upper lip, like a moustache. As I stood up to go, he grabbed me to him and kissed me on the cheek.

I waited till I got outside before I rubbed the Guinness off.

THAT'S OUR COAL

In the dead of winter our Corporation house was icy cold. We'd all huddle up against the fire in the kitchen, trying to keep warm.

"Get back from that fire! Stop sitting on top of it. Let the heat out," Mammy would shout when the fire was low and we hadn't much coal. "If only I could rely on a couple of pounds a week from your father, I'd be well off."

We couldn't call on Mr Campbell any more for turf, and Mammy didn't like going to the new clergyman for help.

I was the only one Mammy trusted to clean out the fire, because I never threw out a single cinder. But when there wasn't even a cinder, any old rubbish would be thrown on to keep it in. Old shoes were a godsend!

Sometimes the fire would be smoking, big black smuts pouring out.

"That chimney needs to be cleaned," Mammy'd say, looking at our eyes all red with the smoke. "Move back all of youse, till I try and clean it."

We'd watch as she'd ruffle up a couple of newspapers, stuff them up the chimney, set fire to them, then open up the black iron damper above the fireplace. The chimney would rumble and roar as the thick caked soot caught fire.

Once there was an unmerciful bang and the red-hot wall

over the fire cracked. We all ran outside to see what was happening. Thick black smoke and sparks were spurting out of our chimney, and Mr Dalton, our neighbour, was staring up at it.

"Jesus, I better put it out," Mammy said, running back in and throwing a basin of water over the fire. "That's it! I think youse all better go to bed, I'm not lighting it again tonight."

The bedrooms were freezing in the winter. They were so cold, Mammy had to wear her overcoat when she was making our beds. My sisters and I would curl up together in bed trying to get a heat off each other.

Our coalman came once a week. I can still see him coming down our road on a cold winter's day. There he'd be, sitting hunched up on his seat behind his horse. His only shelter from the wind and rain was an empty black sack with one corner pushed in, making it into a hood. Another sack lay like a blanket over his knees. His open cart would be piled high with sacks of coal. Young fellas playing in the streets would run, grab hold of the cart and scutt behind.

"Co-aaaal," he'd shout at the top of his voice.

Mammy would rush to the hall door and beckon me in.

"Quick, tell him one bag an', for God's sake, Lily, watch him carrying it in; he's bound to drop some."

Not only did we lose lumps of coal from the top of our open sack, but sometimes there would be holes in the sack itself. And if we weren't quick enough, other children playing in the street would pick these pieces up and run home with them, or else the coalman himself would pick the lumps up on his way out.

"That's our coal," I'd say, jumping on a lump that had fallen out of our sack.

In the front door the coalman would come, bent over with the weight of the heavy sack on his back. Even though Mammy would have hurriedly spread newspapers over our kitchen floor, he'd still leave a trail of wet coal dust from his big old boots all over Mammy's scrubbed floorboards. She would hold open our coal-hole door for him, a dark corner under the stairs in the kitchen. As he emptied the sack, he'd shake it, sending the coal dust blowing back into our kitchen and landing on the table; but we'd be relieved we had some coal once more for the fire.

It puzzled me that no matter what time of the day the coalman came, his face would always be black with coal dust. As he stood silently waiting to be paid, I'd stare at his white, peering eyes. I was curious as to how he managed to hold his wet cigarette butt firmly lodged in the corner of his dirty pink mouth. But how I used to wish he would wipe the drip from the tip of his nose.

"T'anks, Missus," he'd say politely as Mammy counted the right money from her purse. He'd then hurry out as quickly as he could before the children in the street stole coal from the sacks on his cart.

THE EVICTION

It was the early 1940s in old Cabra and everyday life centred around the Catholic church, school and its community. Neighbours went to mass every morning, then stood in groups at corners talking, laughing and gossiping among themselves.

Mammy, being a Protestant, was left out, but religious differences didn't stop us children from playing together. As soon as I came home from school, I was out in the street with all the other children.

Eileen, one of my pals, lived up the road from me in a corner house surrounded by a high hedge. It was great to have a high hedge around your garden. It gave you privacy from neighbours – they wouldn't know all your business.

Eileen's daddy had a steady job and wore a suit to work every day. Each evening he came home at the same time carrying his small case. He never stopped off at the pub, like my daddy did.

At least Daddy won't be makin' a show of me now, comin' home drunk, I thought to myself. Mammy had read in the paper that he was in Mountjoy. He sold sawdust off for tea and got six months for fraud.

I envied Eileen having a daddy who didn't drink and gave up the money. She was always well dressed, and sometimes she even let me try on her black patent-leather hornpipe shoes with large silver buckles. And every winter, she swung around the lamp-post in her brand new shiny black wellingtons.

At night, Eileen and I and the other children would sit under the lamp-post singing the song about the old woman who lived in the woods and killed her baby:

> There was an old woman who lived in the woods,
> Weel-ya, weel-ya, wile-ya,
> There was an old woman who lived in the woods,
> Down by the river Soyl-ya.
>
> She had a baby three months old,
> Weel-ya, weel-ya wile-ya,
> She had a baby three months old,
> Down by the river Soyl-ya.
>
> She had a penknife long and sharp,
> Weel-ya, weel-ya, wile-ya,
> She had a penknife long and sharp,
> Down by the river Soyl-ya.

She stuck the knife in the baby's heart,
Weel-ya, weel-ya, wile-ya,
She stuck the knife in the baby's heart,
Down by the river Soyl-ya.

We'd tell creepy ghost stories that frightened the heart out of us until we were called in to bed.

Unexpectedly, Eileen's daddy died. Mr Cassidy had always done everything for the family. Now Eileen's mammy was left to struggle on her own with five young children.

Eileen began to look shabby. Slowly her house deteriorated. Children broke down parts of her high hedging, squeezed in and ran through the Cassidy's once-lovely garden.

Mrs Cassidy could not cope. She was lonely and began to mix with a group of women whom the neighbours frowned upon: women who wore a lot of make-up, tight skirts and high heels. She started to do herself up and let her long dark hair hang loose. The rouge on her pale little face stood out like two red blotches.

Playing in the street at night with Eileen, I would see her mammy hurrying off to meet her friends in the local pub. Curtains in the houses would lift as she passed by. She brought men home, and they would party all night, singing at the tops of their voices. The men would help her pay her bills.

Then the most shameful thing happened that could ever happen to a woman in those days: Eileen's mammy had a baby with no daddy.

Running through her garden with the other children, I stopped and stared at the blood-stained sheets hanging on the line. Her women friends had delivered her baby.

That was it. Our neighbours took up a petition to have the Cassidy family thrown out. Two women came to our house and asked Mammy to sign it. I was standing behind the door and could hear them giving out hell about her.

"No respectable woman goes to the pub on her own," they

said, shaking their heads. "And that's not all, did ya know she has gone and had a baby out of wedlock?"

When Mammy refused to sign the petition, I was worried.

"Now what's going to happen? Our neighbours will probably tell their children to keep away from me, and I'll have no one to talk to or play with."

My fears were well founded. Next morning, one of my pals walked by me. Lowering her eyes towards my feet, she murmured, "Ahem to the dirt." She was black-out with me.

Hazy rain was falling the morning the men came to evict the Cassidy family. The neighbours stayed indoors. I stood watching silently as the men piled the mattresses one on top of the other next to their furniture in the garden. Their clothes lay scattered in loose bundles on the wet grass.

I ran home to tell Mammy.

"Mammy, it was awful. Missus Cassidy has been thrown out of her home, little baby an' all! An' the mattresses are gettin' all wet in the rain."

"God help her," Mammy said sadly. "What's she going to do? Where are they going?"

"Eileen said they're goin' to live with their granny in the city."

I went over to the window, pulled back the curtain and looked up the road. Eileen and her younger brothers and sisters were walking along carrying what they could. Her mammy followed behind, looking straight ahead, pushing the baby in its go-cart. A horse and cart came a few days later and took away what was left of their belongings. A few of their things had already been stolen.

I never saw Eileen again.

THE HOUSE HAS TO BE MINDED WHEN THE GAS METER'S FULL

He carried a large leather bag, like a doctor's bag. Pushing open our small iron gate, he'd walk briskly up our garden path and knock hard.

"I've come to empty your meter, Missus," he'd say, walking in.

Mammy would breathe a sigh of relief.

"Thank God, before someone else does," she'd say, rushing in after him.

I'd squeeze in before the door closed. Straight into our tiny scullery he'd go, where the big orange meter hung on the cream-distempered wall. While he was reading it, Mammy fussed around, quickly clearing the delph off the kitchen table and brushing down a chair with her hand for him to sit on. Unlocking the big padlock hanging out of the meter, he'd pull out a deep, narrow metal tray crammed full of pennies. By now Annie and Sylvia would have followed me in. We'd all pull our chairs in a little closer as he emptied the pennies with a crash on to our table. In a quick and efficient way, he'd gather the pennies up into stacks of twelve and line them up in front of him. He'd count the stacks, then push several to one side. We'd sit quietly watching him, wondering if the ones he pushed to one side were for Mammy. Reaching for his bag, he'd take out a pile of little brown-paper bags. Dropping a stack of pennies into each one of these bags, he'd fold down the tops carefully, then place them one by one into his leather bag. Without having said one word, he'd stand up, slide the empty tray back into the meter and snap the padlock closed. We'd be too shy to touch the stacks of pennies he'd pushed aside, and held back till he was out the door.

Mammy's face would light up.

"He's left me these because I didn't get enough gas for my pennies," she'd explain.

We had an oilcloth over on our kitchen table. These covers were easy to keep clean and only needed a wipe with a damp cloth after each meal. Ours was white with blue squares. My sisters and I would have great fun playing roll-a-penny into these squares, just like we saw at the Fun Palace in Bray.

"Now we don't have to stay in and mind the house any more while you go for the messages, do we, Mammy?" I'd say, playing with the pennies.

All our neighbours would be in great fear of going out around the time the meters were due to be emptied. So many times we'd hear of someone coming home of an evening, shocked to find their scullery window broken, the meter robbed and the empty tray left lying in the garden.

LITTLE LIZZIE

"I can't be out long, Lily, I have to help me mammy," Maisie would say when I'd call for her.

We'd soon forget about her mammy and run off to play our own special game. First we'd find an iron railings that had the centre bar missing. There was a great one up her back lane. Holding our dresses tightly between our knees, so the boys couldn't see anything, we'd swing over and under, over and under. I loved the way Maisie's long red hair would sweep the ground. When we grew tired of that game, we'd play at jumping over the railings. Whenever Billy Ryan,

Maisie's neighbour, was home from Artane, he'd come out of his house to watch us. I wouldn't jump or swing when he was there even though he'd offer me thrupence.

Maisie's daddy was strict. At night, he'd stand at his hall door and call Maisie and her brothers in, but not by calling their names, like other fathers did. He'd put two fingers in his mouth and let out a loud, sharp whistle. Maisie's brothers would run home from every direction.

"Quick, Maisie! It's your daddy!" we'd all shout, not wanting her to be beaten with the belt of his trousers again.

Her father would often send Maisie to visit her granny, who lived in the basement of a tenement house in the city. She was frightened of going through the dark hall of this strange tenement on her own and would ask me to go with her. When we'd arrive, we'd push open the big hall door right back to the wall, so as to let in as much light as possible. We'd then quickly run through the hall, down dark wooden stairs and into her granny's room.

Although the room was down in a cellar without much light, it had a homely atmosphere and was spotlessly clean. Two cups and saucers stood on a well-scrubbed kitchen table and a black iron kettle hummed on the hob of a well-stacked-up fire. Pictures of ladies in old-fashioned clothes hung on the walls. A heavy polished sideboard dominated this small room. A large glass dome with a stuffed bird inside was placed on top.

Maisie's granny was an invalid and always in bed. Lizzie, a little woman friend, looked after her. Lizzie had no teeth, and her thin lips sunk back into her small face. Her grey hair was pulled back tightly and combed into a bun at the back. She wore a wrap-around flowered apron that was miles too big for her – it almost touched the floor.

While sitting at the table drinking the tea Lizzie had made us, I would look out of her granny's shiny clean window at the well-swept area outside. I could see up to the railings and hear the people talking as they hurried by. Maisie would sit on her granny's bed and tell her all the news about the family. In between fits of coughing, her granny would interrupt her.

"Tell me, Maisie, is yer daddy still workin'? Oh, t'anks be t'God! And how's yer poor mammy? What did she call the new babby? God bless him!"

Maisie's granny would struggle to sit up.

"In the name a' God, Maisie, isn't there any of youse workin' yet and bringin' in a few bob? Yer mammy should be holdin' her apron out by now and youse all should be puttin' money in it."

Lizzie seldom spoke, and whenever she did we could barely hear her. She intrigued me, and all the way home I would want to talk about her.

"Where did Lizzie come from, Maisie? Where's her family? Why does she live with your granny?"

"It's a secret, Lily. Granny found her livin' on the streets years ago and took her home to live with her. Lizzie has never spoken about her past and we know nothin' about her, except that she had been known by the name of Lizzie. Now that granny is bedridden, Lizzie does all the work."

"But what'll happen to Lizzie when your granny dies?"

"Me daddy said she'll come to our house. If we don't take her in, she'd have to go into the Union."

When Maisie's granny died, her daddy inherited all her belongings. I was outside playing when a horse and cart came up our street carrying Maisie's granny's furniture. Next to the furniture sat little Lizzie, clinging to her small bundle of belongings.

Now whenever I'd call for Maisie, I'd see little Lizzie scrubbing the floors and minding the baby. I'd often watch her, as she'd stretch up to hang out the washing. After she'd peg the wet clothes to the line, she would struggle to pull the rope through a pulley to raise it – she'd almost go up with the line herself.

I'd wish we had a little Lizzie to help my mammy.

BY THE SKIN OF HER TEETH

"You're fourteen now, *Lil Ní Shéaghdha*, and I'm afraid you'll have to leave school soon," my teacher said one morning.

I didn't want to leave school, but Mammy didn't have the money to send me on. I had been going to All Saints, a Protestant school in Grangegorman, ever since we moved to Cabra. It was a small school with about forty pupils of all ages. There was only one teacher, Miss Egan. She was slim, wore smart tweed suits, kept her distance and gave little praise. She taught us all in one big cold classroom. We sat in straight rows of desks. A small open fire burned near by where she sat. Every morning, she would march us in a single file around a tiny playground to the tune of "The Grand Old Duke of York".

"This will warm you all up," she'd say, clapping her hands to keep us in time. But my sisters and I would be already warmed up and jaded after running all the way from our home in Cabra.

In the freezing cold mornings of winter, the school caretaker's wife, Mrs Kenny, would push open our school door. In she'd come, carrying a tray laden with small white cups full of hot milk. That was great! We didn't get our milk heated in our last school, St George's.

Our cold hands would curl around the cups as we sipped the hot milk. Miss Egan would stand in front of the fire drinking her milk slowly. The skin from the top of the milk would lodge on her lips. We'd all stare as she skilfully drew it into her mouth with her tongue.

"The skin," she would say quietly, "is the best part of the milk."

The school was close to Grangegorman asylum. One day after school, a few of us wandered down there. We whispered behind its huge grey stone walls. My pals told me a story about the asylum. I made sure to remember it to tell Mammy that evening.

"Once there was a man cyclin' by Grangegorman. He looked up when he heard a voice callin' him from the top of a high wall. It was one of the mad people trying to escape. 'Hey, Mister,' he shouted down, 'will ya please help me get out of here. My wife had me locked up so she could run off with someone else. I swear t'God there's nothin' wrong with me.' 'Okay,' the man with the bike promised, 'I'll be back with a ladder.' As the man was cyclin' away, he got the belt of a brick on the back of his head. Holdin' his head, he picked himself up off the road and looked up at the wall. 'Don't for-gette.... Don't for-gette...,' the man in Grangegorman sang out. We all fell over the path laughin', that was until we heart a sound from the other side of the wall. We went flyin' in case *we* might get the belt of a brick."

Mammy laughed when I told her.

"And guess what else happened, Mammy? When we were passin' the gates of our school on our way home, we saw Miss Egan leavin'. She was walkin' quickly towards Doyle's Corner for her bus, her head in the air, her small attaché case swingin' by her side. And do you know what the O'Byrnes did? They squatted down behind a wall next to our school and waited till she had passed by.

" 'Mary E-gan! Mary E-gan!' they shouted after her. She never looked back. Just imagine, Mammy, she never looked back!"

"Oh God, they'll be in for it tomorrow," Mammy said, looking shocked.

Mammy was right!

The following morning when I arrived at school, Miss Egan was standing at the blackboard, the cane clutched firmly in her hand, her face white with anger. The O'Byrnes came in late, hairs ruffled as if they'd just tumbled out of bed. They glanced at her, then quickly slid into their places. We sat terrified.

Miss Egan shouted at us to own up who called her name out in the street the day before. Two of the O'Byrne brothers got up from their seats, their grey knee socks draped over their boots as they walked up to her.

"How *dare* you call my *name* after me in the street?" Miss Egan said, trembling.

Her cane whistled through the air, landing on their outstretched hands. Fighting hard to hold back the tears, the O'Byrnes marched back to their seats and sat with burning-red faces. In all of the three schools that I went to, I had never felt so frightened as I did that morning when Miss Egan caned these boys so furiously.

Before I left, I sat for the Primary Certificate. It was to help me get a job.

"*Lil Ní Shéaghdha* has passed," Miss Egan announced to the class, "but only by the skin of her teeth!"

LONELY IN CABRA

The gate went. I rushed to the window.

"It's Missus O'Byrne!" I said in alarm.

Mammy made for the door.

"I hope youse don't mind, but I'm going out with her tonight for a drink."

In Mrs O'Byrne came, wearing her husband's loose grey dustcoat swinging open.

"Get your hat an' coat on, O'Shea, we're goin' down to the Hut in Phibsborough," she laughed, plonking herself down in our only armchair.

"I won't be a minute. Just let me comb my hair," Mammy said smiling.

I was sitting at the table trying to sew the crepe sole of my shoe back on with a needle and thread. I hated it flapping when I walked. Mrs O'Byrne looked over at me grimly (I hadn't said hello to her), but nothing could dampen her good humour, and she soon resumed her jokes again and ignored me.

I couldn't understand why Mammy liked her so much. I knew her sons, who went to our school and were for ever in trouble. Only that day Miss Egan had blamed them for the horrible smell in class.

"It's rubber burnin' outside, Miss!" the O'Byrnes replied with a grin.

Miss Egan looked disgusted, and I wondered why she didn't do what Mammy always did! Whenever there was a horrible smell in our room in Fitzgibbon Street, Mammy would stick a small bit of rag in the fire and walk around the room holding it, letting it smoulder. Why didn't Miss Egan think of that?

I was outside playing piggy-beds when Mammy was leaving.

"Go in when Kathleen calls youse, d'ya hear me?" she said softly to me and Annie.

Looking after Mammy with Mrs O'Byrne, I thought how strange they looked together: Mrs O'Byrne so small and round; Mammy so thin beside her. I was worried. I knew what the neighbours thought about women who went to the pub, especially on their own. I hadn't forgotten the eviction of Mrs Cassidy and her children a year ago. Hadn't that started with her going to the pub on her own? But Mrs O'Byrne had a way of lifting Mammy's spirit. She'd be happy for days after.

One day Mammy received a letter from Robbie. In the letter, he said how he wished we lived in an apartment in the city. It would be much easier for him to see us when he'd come home on leave from the navy.

"I tell you what," Mammy said, her face lighting up, "we could look for a transfer. I miss the friendliness of the city. And I wouldn't be sorry to leave that awl fella next door either, him an' his garden, and he's now accusing me of steaming open his letters – as if I would."

"The cheek of him," I muttered angrily. "That's the t'anks we get after bringin' his letters inta him."

Transferring from one Corporation house to another was a common procedure in Dublin. It only required an advertisement in the evening newspaper asking for someone willing to transfer with you. There would be columns of these notices. This exchange had to be approved by the Corporation. After two years of living in Cabra, we moved back to the city.

BENBURB STREET

"Is this it?" we asked, looking up at the high, grey, dismal concrete building in Benburb Street.

There was a whole street of these buildings. They had been built by the Corporation to help ease the overcrowding of large families living in tenements. Our flat, 2B, was situated on the second floor. Women wearing black shawls stood around the main hall door suspiciously watching us coming in and out. The hall was cold, drab and stank of urine – there was a pub at the corner. Mammy tried to see the positive side to the move.

"Listen, it's not so bad really. I know we haven't got our own lavatory, but there's one on every landing. And look at this nice big range; the place will get lovely and warm in winter."

The sound of shouting and fighting in the street drew us all over to the dirty window. We stared down.

"Besides," Mammy added quietly, "we can keep to ourselves."

The back window of this kitchen looked out on to a roof of a house behind us. At night, the stray cats of the city would jump from the roof on to our windowsill and stare in with their wild, scabby eyes. They'd hiss at us when we'd bang off the window. Next morning, when we'd pull up the window, a stench of cat pee would drift into our kitchen.

I was no longer at school and tried to stay out of the flat as much as I could. I made friends with the other children close by. Every morning, we'd go off and explore the city. I saw Bang Bang again. He was still jumping on and off buses shouting, "Bang, bang," pretending to shoot people with a key. Friendly buskers playing accordions were everywhere.

We'd visit the museum on Parnell Square. It'd be deathly

quiet inside. We'd have to whisper and tiptoe around. The attendant would keep an eye on us, but when he wasn't looking, we'd peep under the sheets that were draped over the nude statues of men and women.

The Fun Palace on the quays was another great attraction. Colourful posters displayed on the wall outside invited us to come in and see the smallest woman in the world or the beautiful Siamese twin girls. We didn't have the money, but that didn't stop us from staring at the posters and using our imaginations.

My pals would seldom pass a chapel without a visit. Fed up waiting outside, I'd slip in after them. Here and there, men and women would be kneeling in devoted prayer, fingering their rosary beads. The women would have their heads covered with a scarf or hat, but men would always remove their caps on entering. Statues were placed around the church in dimly lit corners, some with a vase of flowers in front. Now and again, people would kneel down and pray in front of them; other people walked softly up the church towards a stand where dozens of small white candles flickered. When one candle burnt itself out, it would be quickly replaced. A penny clinked into a box as they paid for it.

"The candles are burning for departed souls," my pals would whisper to me.

I felt strange in these big churches. The sickly scent of flowers and incense made me feel dizzy.

After a few minutes, my pals would bless themselves, stand up and genuflect in the aisle. Then leaving the church, they'd dip their fingers in a huge holy water font and bless themselves again.

Coming home tired of an evening, we'd saunter alongside the Liffey wall. Leaning over, we'd look down at the water and watch the slippery, slimy muck that floated by. The murky water would lap against the black scum on the wall. A brown, frothy stuff would float back up on to the surface. The stench of the Liffey would waft up to us.

We'd know it was late when we'd see crowds of cyclists weaving their way in between buses down O'Connell Street, on their way home from work. As we ran, we'd kick out at old newspapers that blew around our feet and stamp on lighted butts that glowed red on the path.

Climbing the stairs of our block of flats, I'd hear children screaming behind one of the doors and the sound of delph breaking against the wall as their parents fought. I'd hurry by in case the door opened. Living in Benburb Street brought back memories of my own experiences with my father when we were living in Fitzgibbon Street.

A BED ALL TO MYSELF

I stepped off the bus in Dún Laoghaire carrying my small suitcase. The clergyman from our new parish, St Paul's, had found me a job. I was to help look after a baby for a young curate's wife.

"You'll have a lovely room and a bed all to yourself," Mammy had reassured me.

The curate's house was next door to a small Protestant church. I closed the big black iron gates nervously behind me and tried to walk quietly up the gravel path towards the house. I knocked softly. The door opened almost immediately.

"You must be Lily O'Shea," the curate's wife said smiling.

Then taking my case from me, she welcomed me inside. We walked down a long hall which was covered with a thick, narrow carpet that continued up the stairs – it felt really posh. I thought how pretty she looked in her blue cotton dress. I glanced at my old faded dress that had been passed down to me from Kathleen.

The room was immaculate with its small bed and wardrobe. Not knowing what to do, I sat down on the edge of the bed and touched its sloping ceiling. A feeling of loneliness came over me.

That evening I met the curate. He smiled and shook hands with me. Before I went to bed, I was instructed that every morning after breakfast, I was to take the baby out in his pram for a couple of hours before dinner. I enjoyed these trips. The baby was one year old, placid and no trouble. Holding the white bone handle of this high black English pram, I pushed it proudly. It just bounced along.

I thought back of the old prams in the tenements that I used to wheel. Their springs were slack from being overloaded and the wonky wheels were for ever spinning off on to the road. The babies were reared in the prams – some even slept in them overnight.

While wheeling the pram along Dún Laoghaire's Regal Promenade, I'd stop and stare at the mailboats sailing in and out of the harbour. Other times, I'd go for walks down quiet tree-lined streets and peep through the large iron gates at the huge redbrick houses. On my way back to the curate's house, I'd pass groups of girls dawdling home from college carrying their books. They'd be laughing and joking with each other, flicking their striped scarves over their shoulders.

A few days after I arrived, the curate's wife asked me to scrub the bathroom floorboards.

"That's excellent, Lily. You are very good at scrubbing!"

Slowly the jobs increased. I now not only had to mind the baby, but had to polish the furniture and clean out the fire as well. Then one morning the curate's wife called me downstairs and asked me to try on an old black dress with a white collar. My heart sank when I saw it. It was a maid's dress.

"I don't t'ink it fits me," I said, praying to God that she wouldn't make me wear it. "It's swimmin' on me; it's down to me ankles!"

"I know it's a little big for you, Lily. It was made for my last girl. She was from the country."

I was told to put the dress on of an evening, and every time I heard the knocker to come down, open the door and usher the visitor into the parlour. Then I was to return to my room.

I missed Mammy dreadfully. I had no one to talk to. When I'd be out the baby in the pram, I would look for a secluded seat, take him out and hug him for comfort. At night, I would sit in my room and look out of its tiny window wondering what my sisters were doing.

How lucky Kathleen is, I thought to myself, *workin' as a waitress in Caffollas's ice-cream parlor. She can go home every evenin'. I suppose they're sittin' around the fire talkin' and laughin', and I'm here all on my own.*

I'd wake up in the middle of the night and have to rush to the bathroom and vomit.

At the end of the second week, I was allowed to return home for the weekend with my five shillings, my wages. My sisters asked me how I liked my new job.

"It's great! I love it. I have a bed all to myself in my own room with lovely white sheets, and I can have a bath with hot water. I don't have to heat up pots and pots of water on their cooker to put in the bath, like you do. It's already there."

I kept up this pretence all weekend, but when it was time for me to leave home and return I broke down and sobbed. Mammy did not look surprised.

"You don't have to go back, love. I'll send Kathleen to fetch your case and apologise to the curate and his wife."

YOUNG SEAN

"There's young Sean coming home from work," Mammy would say, glancing towards our door.

We'd be having our tea when we'd hear the slow thud of Sean's boxcar wheels on the concrete stairs as he dragged it up to his door. Sean was thirteen and lived on the same floor as us.

His father had made him a boxcar out of a large butter box. It had two small pram wheels in front and two narrow wooden laths for handles to push.

Sean would leave home early every morning with his boxcar and come home late in the evening. My pals told me he collected rags, then sold them to the city rag dealers. Whenever I'd pass him on the stairs, he would keep his head down, squinting up at me under his eyes. Hunched up he'd be, in his thin little coat that went right up his back, with hair that looked as if it had never seen a comb.

One night we all woke up to loud, pitiful screams coming from Sean's flat across our landing. I lay there shaking with fright. Mammy came and sat on our bed.

"It sounds like poor Sean's being beaten. God help him. Try an' go back to sleep."

Next morning, when Mammy and I were coming out of our door, Sean's mother was also leaving.

"Hello, Missus!" she called over to Mammy. "Did ya hear that young fella a'mine screamin' last night? The little bugger, robbin' me he was!"

Mammy nodded coldly and made for the stairs. Hurrying down after us, Sean's mother persisted on telling Mammy the whole story.

"Wait till I tell ya, Missus. Him an' me heard young Sean talkin' in his sleep last night, sayin' he'd kep' back money

168

from us. 'Where is it, son? Where's it hidden?' I kep' askin'. Still half asleep, he told me. I was out a' bed like a flash an' went through the bucket a'slack next to me fire. An' Jesus, Mary and Joseph, Missus, I found a half a crown, a half a crown!"

"My God, we'll have to try and get back to Cabra," Mammy whispered, pulling me out the front door. "Robbie was right. It's a terrible place; certainly not an apartment; worse than the tenements."

SHE'S NOT SOFT LIKE YOU, MAMMY

What a shock we had when we transferred back to a Corporation house in Drumcliffe Road, Cabra West. Daddy was living on the same road with another woman. They had two children. It was Sylvia who ran in and told us.

"Mammy, I saw Daddy. He lives just 'round the corner of our road in another house. He says he's comin' 'round to see us."

Mammy went white and had to sit down.

"Jesus, are you sure? Going into another house, what kind of a house? So that's where he's been."

"Yes, he says he lives there now with someone else."

I looked out the window.

"It must be the same woman, Mammy. The one he was seein' when we lived in Fitzgibbon Street, when Kathleen and I followed him one night?"

After a few minutes, Mammy jumped up, started scrubbing the floorboards and hanging up our old curtains.

"Thank God for Robbie's few bob," she said quietly.

I felt ashamed and angry with my father living so close to us with someone else, but secretly I was glad. We would not have to put up with him and his drinking any more.

That night, my father rushed around to see us, as if we were old friends. Even though Mammy was terribly hurt and upset, she let him in. He was full of apologies.

"When I came out of the Joy, I couldn't find youse. I went bangin' off the house in old Cabra. They wouldn't tell me where youse went."

Daddy looked strange, pale and thinner, and spoke out of the corner of his mouth. He laughed at his own jokes and the tricks he had played on other prisoners in the exercise yard in Mountjoy, and he called the wardens "screws". Annie and I didn't understand him and stood back as he spat in the fire.

Mammy told him all about our experiences in Benburb Street and how we had to stay there for six months before the Corporation would consider us for another transfer.

"Still, you've got a lovely house here anyway, another kitchen house with three bedrooms," he said, looking around smiling.

Sylvia kept interrupting him.

"Daddy, d'ya know the woman who used to live here? Well, she had millions of children and a great big fat belly. Like this, Daddy! Look, Daddy, like this," she said pulling her jumper up and pushing her stomach out.

My father roared with laughter as he grabbed Sylvia up. Mammy's eyes shone, and I could see once more she had forgiven him.

From then on, my father would often call in and stay for a while chatting to Mammy and tricking around with us, but he didn't want to hear about bills or how she was managing. He never offered her a penny. I met him on the 22 bus one day as I was going into the GPO to post Mammy's letter to Robbie.

"Here, I'll pay for her," my father said to the conductor, handing him my fare.

I was delighted. But as soon as we got off the bus to go our separate ways, he came up close to me, held out his hand and said, "Can ya give me back that money!"

Some nights, he'd stagger around drunk.

"I love ya, Doll, I love ya," he'd whine, hanging out of Mammy.

She'd give him something to eat, then half carry him up to bed – just like she always did in old Cabra. When she'd come back down, her face would be red from his unshaven chin.

"Why do you let him in?" I'd snap. "Let her put up with him."

"Don't be so hard on him, Lily. He's good really, just easily led," Mammy would say, straightening her apron.

Sitting in front of the fire, my feet on our fender, I would poke the fire hard, sending up sparks.

"Well, he's makin' a holy show of us comin' around here when he's drunk. She's not soft like you, Mammy; she wouldn't let him in."

My Last Year at Roseville

"I can't go to Roseville," Mammy said firmly. "I couldn't leave Johnny on his own. He's gone eleven, and they don't allow boys after ten."

Mammy looked over at me.

"You can't go either, Lily, you're gone fourteen! Girls are not allowed after fourteen."

"Well, why can't you let on that I'm not fourteen yet?" I pleaded. "Annie and I could go together."

Mammy picked up the form and read it again. Our clergyman, Mr Jenkins, needed to know soon.

"Yes, g'wan, Mammy, they'll never know. I want to go too!" Sylvia begged.

"Mammy, just write down that I'm only thirteen," I said quietly, "then the three of us can go."

"I wish you wouldn't make me do this," Mammy sighed, as she filled in the form.

At last the day came, and we were going to Roseville – Annie, Sylvia and I.

Roseville, a lovely old home in Bray, was owned by the Protestant diocese of Dublin to give their parishioners a holiday they could never afford. Mothers in need of a rest would be given a bright airy room for themselves and their children to sleep in. Fathers were not allowed to stay, but could visit and often did. We knew when somebody's daddy was visiting. The children would be sent out of the room, the curtains drawn and the keys turned in the locks.

Mammy carried our case to the bus stop, then grabbed hold of my arm.

"Now listen to me, Lily! You and Annie have to mind Sylvia. She can't walk very far since she fell off that big bike, and she is only nine. D'ya hear me?"

After what seemed like a long journey, the bus stopped outside Roseville. I felt so happy pushing open the big wooden gate and struggling with our case up the winding path to the house. I wanted to touch the walls that ran along each side of the narrow path and caress their stones that were of every shape and size.

Miss Irwin, the matron, was standing at the door chatting

to mothers who were sitting knitting on long wooden seats. Colourful buckets and spades covered with sand were thrown underneath.

"You must be the O'Shea girls," she said, taking our case.

Miss Irwin was a small, slim, elderly spinster with short curly grey hair neatly pinned back from her face – a kind face that never seemed to change from year to year. She showed us upstairs to a small dormitory with six single beds. A wash-stand stood under one of the windows with a basin and a jug of water. Our clothes stayed in our case next to our beds.

Miss Irwin lived in rooms at the back of the house with her two Pekinese dogs. She told us the times of our meals and when we were expected to be in bed by; otherwise we were free to come and go as we pleased.

First we explored the front and back gardens, hoping nothing had changed. We had lots of secret hiding places in these gardens. We knew every corner, and they held a kind of magic for us. Down the front path we ran and found the narrow stone steps that led up to a small secluded garden surrounded by trees and bushes. A mother was sitting here on an old wooden seat reading. We left her in peace and hurried around to the orchard at the back of the house to see if the rope swing that squeaked as you swung was still there.

Then, full of excitement, we headed down to the sea. As we passed a sweets factory, we stopped, sniffed and savoured its hot toffee-like smell. It was nearly as good as eating a sweet.

We had to cross rail tracks to get to the sea. The big white crossing gates were closed. A narrow iron bridge with steep steps crossed over the tracks. When Mammy was with us, we'd walk over this bridge, but now, on our own, we scrambled up on to the gates singing:

> There's a grasshopper sitting on the railway tracks,
> Singing polly wolly doodle all the day.

I come from Louisiana to meet my Suzianna
Singing polly wolly doodle all the day.

Hanging on to the gates, we had a free ride as they opened.

The whole sea front was full of life. A long promenade with railings stretched along the stony seashore to Bray Head. We climbed up on the railings and jumped back down, squealing as the waves crashed in and washed over. Mothers and nannies with their big high prams were sitting on a long wooden seat enjoying the breeze from the sea.

Leaving the promenade, we skipped down several stone steps to a wide grass area and ran towards a kiosk selling ice cream cornets. Bunches of colourful tin buckets and spades were hanging each side of its little windows. As we passed, Sylvia stretched up and touched one.

"I wish I had one of those," she begged.

"Well, we haven't got any money to buy one," I answered. "Oh look, Sylvia, there's a show going on at the bandstand."

Up on the stage, actors were telling jokes we didn't understand, but the men looking on did; they were falling around laughing. We enjoyed the end of the show – that was the best bit – when the actors danced and sang and encouraged us all to join in singing, "Zippity doo dah, zippity day. My oh my, what a wonderful day." The sound of laughter sent us running towards the amusements. Someone had put a penny in the slot of the jolly fat policeman, making him shake and roar with laughter.

"Excuse me, Mister, d'ya have the time please?" I asked a man passing by.

"It's a quarter t'six, love."

I panicked.

"God, we'd better run or we'll be late for tea!"

"I can't run wit' me sore knee," Sylvia whinged, hobbling behind us.

Annie and I dragged her along for as far as we could, then

174

we had to carry her in between us. Matron was ringing the bell as we pushed open the gate and stumbled in.

We scurried around the back to an outside tap to wash our hands. On our way, we peeped into the dining room windows. A long table was set with plates of thick sliced homemade brown bread and butter. Bees were buzzing around the small dishes of blackberry jam.

"Come along in, you three girls, and sit down," Matron said as we entered.

Mothers with their children beside them were smiling happily. The babies didn't know themselves, sitting up in big wooden high chairs. Sweet milky tea in colourful nursery-rhyme mugs were placed in front of us. How delicious the blackberry jam tasted on the fresh brown bread!

Two other girls slept in our dormitory; they were pals and kept to themselves. They told us their parents had gone to France on holiday. We admired their pretty dresses and thought how well off they must be.

Feeling happy and content with our day, we lay in bed quietly listening to Matron calling one of her dogs in for the night.

"Barney! Barney! Barney!" she sang out in her soft posh voice.

When the bell rang for breakfast, we ran down the stairs into the dining room and sat in our places. We were each handed a big bowl of porridge.

"There's jugs of hot milk on the table, girls, and bowls of brown sugar," Matron said, "and if you want more porridge there's plenty."

"And where are youse girls off to t'day?" one of the mothers called over to us as we dug into the brown sugar and shovelled it on thick.

"We're goin' down the back strand to collect chaneys," Sylvia said excitedly.

"Don't forget dinner at one o'clock," Matron reminded us as we rushed out the door.

Down we ran towards the back strand, singing:

> Zippity doo dah, zippity day.
> My oh my, what a wonderful day.
> Plenty of sunshine coming our way.
> Zippity doo dah, zippity day.

A long quiet road led into the back strand where the tinkers – or gypsies, as we called them – lived in their colourful round wooden caravans. Broken prams, iron bed ends and other scrap metal were scattered near by. The women looked grubby in old boots and shabby long skirts, squatting in front of smoky fires on the sand. They watched us silently with sharp eyes. The children ran around in raggedy old woollens and wellingtons. Ignoring them and their runny noses, we kept well away and busily collected small pieces of coloured glass or delph made smooth by the sand and the sea – our chaneys. We were used to gypsies knocking on our door at home selling pegs and paper flowers and asking Mammy to cross their hand with silver while they told her fortune. Mammy would never refuse them in case they wished her bad luck. We didn't stay here long. It was too quiet and frightening.

After dinner, we went back down to the sea front. Tucking the hems of our dresses under the elastic at the legs of our knickers, we splashed along the edge of the sea. Picking up a stick, I wrote my name on the damp sand.

Two local boys came along.

"Is that your name?" they asked, stopping.

Annie and I quickly pulled down our dresses.

"Well, what's your names?" we asked shyly.

Laughing and joking, we climbed to the top of Bray Head with Tommy and Colin. Coming down, Sylvia skidded and slipped on the damp gritty path. She refused to get up and started crying.

"I'm not walkin' any more, so I'm not. And when Mammy comes on Saturday with our clean clothes, I'm goin' to tell her on youse for bein' with boys!"

We were about half an hour's walk away from Roseville, and Annie and I knew we'd have to hurry if we were to make it for tea. Tommy bent down.

"C'mon, Sylvia, I'll give you a piggy-back."

Grinning, she jumped up, grabbed his neck and wrapped her skinny bruised legs around his waist.

We saw the boys every day after that and would meet up with them again after tea, but made sure to be back in by nine o'clock to have our hot cocoa with the mothers in the dining room.

I had to hold back the tears on the morning we were leaving. I knew it was my last year at Roseville. We left after our porridge with hot milk and brown sugar. Tommy and I had arranged to meet outside the Fun Palace in Dublin one week later. The thought of seeing him again cheered me up.

I came in on the bus to meet him wearing my new beige coat. As I approached the Fun Palace, I saw Tommy sitting on his bike talking to a girl. He didn't recognise me. I walked by him and went home.

"You silly little fool, you," Mammy said, when I arrived home upset. "He had cycled all the way in from Bray to see you and you walked by him."

I Thought You Wouldn't Mind

Patrick was a tall, skinny boy of fifteen with straight brown hair, well oiled. I liked the way he looked at me and smiled, a warm, friendly smile that moved me.

All through the autumn, Patrick and I would ramble out into the countryside towards Finglas. He'd walk at the edge of the path, I'd walk on the inside. Now and again, we'd stop and sit on a low stone wall and talk.

One Sunday afternoon, Johnny followed behind pestering us.

"Where are ya goin', Lily? Where are ya goin'?" he kept shouting.

Patrick became annoyed. He went back to my brother and tried to persuade him to leave us alone.

"Here, if I give you this, will you go home?" Patrick said, taking his sling out of his back pocket.

His eyes lighting up, Johnny grabbed it. He never had such a sling before. This was a big boy's sling, a real one. Picking up a stone, he tried it out.

"Oh great, t'anks," he said, stuffing it into his pocket and galloping off, his hand hitting his behind, as if on a horse.

While sauntering back home past the Corporation houses on Rathoath Road, I happened to look up at a bedroom window. A little boy was standing up in his cot. He had pulled the curtains up over his head, and I could see that he had no napkin on. Patrick put his hands over my eyes, laughing with me as he did so.

After a few weeks, I gave him a snap of me standing at our hall door. Patrick put it in the inside pocket of his jacket very carefully.

"T'anks," he said proudly, patting his pocket.

Feeling sure of him, I thought this was the right moment to tell him something that was worrying me.

"You know I'm not a Catholic," I blurted out quickly.

He dropped my hand and stared at me.

"Ya're not a Catholic! Ya're a Protestant?" he said with a look of disbelief on his face. "Why didn't ya tell me that before now?"

"I thought you wouldn't mind!"

"Well, I'll have ya know, Lily O'Shea, that me father is fightin' to free Ireland, and he would be shocked if he knew I was seein' a Protestant girl – and so would me mam."

He took out my snap and tore it up into small pieces. I watched the shiny white pieces fluttering slowly down to the ground. Biting my lip and fighting back the tears, I bent down and gathered up the bits. Without looking back at him, I ran all the way home and sobbed.

THE CLERGYMAN'S LETTER

"No, Mammy! I'm not going after any more of those 'Smart Girl Wanted' jobs in that paper," I said, trying to poke a bit of life into the fire.

Mammy screwed up the newspaper hard and threw it into the coal bucket. Her chair scraped on the lino as she stood up.

"Get up from the fire, Lily! I'm fed up looking at you sitting on top of it. Look at Annie. She's got herself a good job in a small factory."

Untying her apron, she threw it on the back of a chair.

"Come on," she said, "comb your hair and get your coat

on! We're going down to see Mr Jenkins – see if he'll give you a letter that might get you in somewhere."

Pulling her coat on, she headed for the door.

Mammy knew that a letter from a clergyman could help you get work in one of the many Protestant factories around Dublin in the 1940s. But as Mr Jenkins didn't come near us, she was reluctant to ask him for help, unless it was really necessary.

Mr Jenkins' house was set behind my old school and church in Grangegorman. We opened up the small wooden gate and cut through the schoolyard. Our shoes crunched on his long pebbly driveway as we walked up towards his big house, and his dogs started barking. I moved closer to Mammy and linked her arm. She kept walking, saying nothing, just staring straight in front, one hand holding her coat across her. The door opened just as we got to it.

"How can I help you, Mrs O'Shea?" Mr Jenkins said.

He stood aside and waved a hand, directing us into his parlour. He was wearing his black clergyman clothes with his white collar. I noticed how his nose looked long and sharp on his thin face. I tried to pull my coat down to cover my skirt as I followed Mammy inside.

Mammy explained to him why we had come. He left us standing and went into another room. We didn't like to sit down on his lovely polished chairs. Several minutes later, he returned and handed her a sealed envelope.

"This should get her into Burton's, Mrs O'Shea," he said, walking us to the door.

We hurried down the driveway and Mammy took hold of my arm. She was happy.

"Come on, love, we won't walk back home. Let's get the bus!"

STAND UP FOR YOURSELF

It was my first morning in Burton's. I quickly dressed, dashed for the 7.15 bus and collapsed on a seat upstairs, panting. The bus sped across the city over to the south side. I jumped off in Camden Street and hurried down the Long Lane into New Street and Burton's.

Two big wooden gates were wide open, their pink paintwork faded and scratched. Men and women cycled around me, across the cobbled yard towards a bicycle shed. I was taken though the factory, a huge room full of noisy sewing machines and steaming Hoffman Pressers, into the cutting room.

At least six men and a red-headed boy worked in the cutting room. It was a brightly lit room with no windows, quiet compared to the factory. Occasionally, the men would whistle softly to themselves as they snapped away with their scissors.

My job was to collect bundles of material from the cutters and write down the numbers into a large book. A kind elderly foreman kept an eye on my book, noting the number of suits the men were cutting out. The bundles were then sent out into the factory to a forewoman who would hand them out to the girls on the machines to be made up.

I was delighted to be getting fifteen shillings a week. I'd give Mammy my pay packet, and she'd give me a few shillings back for myself. But it was lonely in the cutting room with no other girl to talk to. Soccer, boxing and horse racing was all the men talked about.

Willie, the red-headed boy who was being trained as a cutter, was expected to run messages for the men. One of his jobs was to go down the cellar and fetch the men their chalks. He hated doing this.

"You have to go down the cellar, Lily O'Shea, and get the men their chalks. I was here before you were!" he said.

"That's your job, Willie McEvoy!" I protested, not looking up at him.

"Go on! Get them!" he shouted, pointing to the far corner of the cutting room.

My hands shook as I closed my book and dropped my pencil on top. I took my time walking towards the entrance of the cellar, all the while sensing Willie close behind me. I hesitated at the top of the steep wooden stairs.

"Go on then!" he snapped.

Each step I took down, I could feel it getting colder. A musty smell drifted up to me. It was deathly quiet but for the low drone of the sewing machine motors in the factory above. Narrow passages separated rows of tall dusty shelves where boxes of chalks and threads were kept. Slowly I made my way down each dark, shadowy passageway, searching for the shelf where the chalks were kept.

Oh t'ank God, there it is!

Grabbing one of the boxes, I dashed back across the concrete floor and up the stairs to where Willie was waiting. He took the box from me and, with a smile on his face, rushed on ahead and gave them to the men as if he had fetched them!

Every night I'd come home upset and snap at my sisters for nothing at all. Mammy got fed up with me.

"Has that boy made you go down the cellar again?" she asked me one night, staring across the table at my untouched dinner. "For God's sake, Lily, stand up for yourself!" she said firmly. "Don't do what he says! I'll tell you what to say, and he won't go near you again."

The very next day Willie tried to send me down the cellar again. I stood up and looked at him, my heart thumping.

"When I started in this job, Willie McEvoy, I was told who was over me – and you weren't one of them!"

I couldn't believe it: Mammy was right. He walked away!

In Between

"Jesus, Lily! Get up! You're dead late! The alarm on the clock didn't go off."

"Oh no, Mammy, not again! What time is it?"

Throwing my clothes on, I'd run down the stairs.

"Where's me coat and scarf?" I'd whine, hurrying into the kitchen.

The bus driver would see me running, start up the engine and pull out slowly – letting on he was going without me.

I became bored in the cutting room jotting down numbers and began to wander around chatting to the men. The foreman caught me one day. I ducked down, but wasn't quick enough.

"Miss O'Shea," he called out loudly, "will you please stand up and go back to your table."

The men looked up and roared with laughter. I walked back to my place, my face red and burning.

The men were fond of a laugh and often cracked jokes with each other – especially on a Friday when they'd be looking forward to the weekend.

"Still no girlfriend, Mick?" one of the married men would call over to a single fella.

Mick was an amateur boxer, shy and not interested in girls.

"You don't know what you're missing," they'd say, winking at each other.

Not all the single fellas were shy like Mick. Whenever they wanted to date a girl, they'd wait till the foreman left the room, then beckon me over to them.

"Quick, Lily, can you run out into the factory and give this note to a girl for me? C'mere till I show you her?" he'd say, bringing me over to the doorway that led into the factory.

"Look, there she is on the buttonhole machine; she's standing up threading it."

"Yes, I see her. Give me the note! I'll go," I'd say, feeling envious. I wished I were in the factory like these girls with their little handbag mirrors propped up in front of their machines to powder their faces.

I'd slip out with the note. The girl would quickly read it, then look towards the cutting room door, smile and nod. Other times, the men made the dates themselves as they passed through the factory to the lavatory.

"I'm going for a smoke, Mick," Joe would call out, putting down his chalks.

Joe'd comb his hair, spit on his hands and press his quiff into place. Satisfied, he'd stand and brush down the dusty chalk marks all over his trousers. Straightening his tie, he'd walk briskly out of the cutting room and into the factory. As he passed rows of girls, he'd slow up near one and drop a note on her machine. If the girl was interested, she'd read it and scribble out a reply for him to pick up on his way back.

Coming back into the cutting room, he'd be whistling, "Just Molly and me, and baby makes three, were happy in my blue heaven." The men would smile at each other knowingly, and for the rest of the afternoon, we'd hear nothing else but his whistle.

Every year Burton's ran a dance for their employees. The men talked about nothing else for weeks beforehand.

"You'll have to go to the dance this year, Lily, it's great," Joe called over to me.

I was a little nervous. This was my first dance, so I asked Annie to come along with her boyfriend. He was the tailor in the factory where she worked. She used to confide in me at night about him.

"I hear him doing Spanish dancin' in the room above me,"

she'd whisper. So I knew if Annie brought her boyfriend along, I'd be all right for a dance.

I needn't have worried. The men from the cutting room came over, one after the other, and asked me up.

"Don't look down at your feet, just follow me," they'd say as they twirled me round the floor of the National Ballroom.

The highlight of the night was a performance by the Irish dancer Rory O'Connor. Dressed in his full Irish costume, he danced on the centre of the floor. He held his head high, his back straight and his hands firmly by his side. His feet tapped on the floor in perfect time to each Irish number the band played.

Lying in bed that night, I thought about the dance. *Movin' around the floor to the slow beat of the drums was great. Once I got into the rhythm, it was easy. I can't wait to go again.*

Monday morning, I sat on my stool happily writing in my numbers listening to the men joking with each other about the dance.

"See you got your mark off, Mick?" they laughed.

Mick ignored them. Joe looked over at me and smiled.

"Did you enjoy the dance, Lily? I'm a great dancer, aren't I?"

I tried hard to stop my face from blushing.

WHAT COULD SHE BE CONFESSIN'?

One day on my way to work, I sat beside a girl on the bus who lived on the same street as me. We sat chatting and realised we both worked in Burton's.

"What do you do? Are you on a machine in the factory?" I asked her.

185

"No, I'm not on a machine. I stand behind a table and soap the bottom of trousers before they are turned up and pressed."

"I wish I was out in the factory. I haven't got anyone to talk to in the cuttin' room!"

She looked at me.

"Well, when you're passin' by on your way to the lavatory, you can stop and talk to me. The forewoman is great. She won't say anythin'."

"I'll see you at lunchtime," I called back happily as I left her and hurried up into the cutting room.

All morning I looked forward to seeing her. As soon as I heard the machines slow down and stop, I quickly finished writing out the numbers in my book and put it on a shelf underneath my table. Carrying my coat and lunch, I rushed out of the cutting room ahead of the men. Maura was standing at her table holding her coat, looking towards the cutting room, smiling.

After we had eaten in the canteen, we decided to go for a walk. Slipping our coats and scarves on, we left Burton's and walked happily down New Street, a narrow street with a few shabby white-washed cottages squashed in between a number of dilapidated factory gates. The dust blew up in our faces as open-back lorries and horses and carts rumbled by. We hadn't walked far when we came across St Patrick's Church. We wandered into its small garden. Tucking our coats under us, we sat down on a damp wooden seat. It was peaceful and quiet here, away from the busy traffic. St Patrick's was a Protestant church. Catholic children played on the path outside. Maura looked up at the church and then at me.

"You're a Protestant, Lily, aren't you?" she said. "I knew you were, because you're on the office staff. You've got a good job in the cuttin' room."

We sat for a moment without saying anything.

"Let's have our lunch here tomorrow?" I said eagerly, wanting to change the subject. "I don't like the canteen, do you? An' I don't like drinkin' out of those big white mugs, an' some of them are even chipped and cracked. An' I don't like the women servin'. They only talk to the men, don't they? Oh God, Maura, it's gettin' late, we'd better go. C'mon!"

We hurried back to the factory. All afternoon, I thought about what Maura had said about me being a Protestant and on the office staff. I never saw any of the girls from the office, except on a Friday, which was pay day. A girl would come into the cutting room carrying a tray of pay packets, walk by me and hand them to the foreman, who'd give them to the workers. She was tall, slim, held her head high and wore a tight red hand-knitted jumper, which emphasised her pointy breasts. All the men would stop working and whistle loudly after her. She'd smile, but never looked near them, nor me.

Maura told me next morning that she could have lunch with me in St Patrick's garden. On our way, we passed a small dairy and bought a large bottle of milk between us.

"Let's not shake the bottle," I said, pulling the red and white cardboard top off and licking it. "We'll take turns. I'll have the cream today and you can have it tomorrow."

Maura and I became good pals. She called for me every morning; most times I'd be late.

"Oh there's Maura at the door, Mammy," I'd whine, pulling the rag curlers out of my hair.

"Here, eat your fried bread and I'll let her in."

Every Saturday evening I went with Maura to confession. With our arms linked together, we'd walk down to St Peter's Church in Phibsborough.

"C'mon in," she'd say when I'd hesitate at the church door.

Before entering, we'd put our head scarves on. She'd dip her fingers in a concrete holy water font and bless herself.

"Wait there," she'd whisper, pointing to a seat at the back of the church.

Here and there in this silent church, small groups of people would be kneeling in front of their seats patiently waiting in a queue for their turn to confess their sins. Maura would kneel down beside them. When it was her turn, I'd watch as she got up and slipped in through a narrow door.

What could she be confessin'? I'd wonder to myself.

"Maura, what do you tell the priest in confession?" I asked her one week while leaving.

"Oh, you know, Lily. Anythin' I have done wrong. And if I have not got any sins, I tell him my past sins."

"What sort of past sins?" I asked her seriously.

"Oh, Lily, you know: disobedient to my father, or late for mass. Those kinds of things."

We'd walk to a chip shop near the Bohemian picture house, sit on a wooden bench inside and order a fourpenny ice cream. It was served in a dish with a wafer on top. Chatting and laughing, we'd saunter back home. She had to be in by nine o'clock.

I did the "seven chapels" with Maura and I began going with her to the "miraculous medal" on a Monday night, a devotion to Our Lady for Catholic women. The chapel would be packed out to the doors, and we'd seldom get a seat. I found the last hymn very moving:

> Oh Mary conceived without sin,
> Oh Mary conceived without sin,
> Pray for us,
> Pray for us,
> Who have recourse to thee.

Listening to the women's voices as they sang this hymn with so much feeling, my eyes would fill up.

Then Maura met a boy that she liked, and began seeing him all her free time, so I no longer went to confession or the miraculous medal with her.

"I'll see you on Monday," she'd call back to me on a Friday after work.

I missed her and had no pal to go out with. Then she left Burton's to work with her sister in Lever's, a soap factory.

"I don't really want to go," she said, "but I'll get more money."

Maura and I didn't see each other much after that. But thinking back, I would have done the same. It was the kind of thing we often did then. When we met a boy we liked, we dropped our girlfriend.

AT HOME IN THE FACTORY

"You won't always be in the cutting room, Lily, you know. You will eventually be moved up into the office. Not every girl gets that opportunity. Remember the clergyman's letter got you *that* job!"

"Mammy, I have been there nearly two years and I haven't been promoted into the office. I don't even like the girls in the office. I know they're Protestants, but they're different to me: they're well off, and they speak posh. Besides I will get much more money out in the factory! At least two pounds a week, and I'll be able t'give you more."

My transfer came through. I had to start right at the bottom with the new girls, running messages for the machinists. However, it was not very long before the forewoman sat me down in front of a sewing machine and showed me how to sew a straight seam. I was put beside a girl called Bridie. Our job was to join the legs of men's trousers.

As we sewed, Bridie and I laughed and talked non-stop. Every Monday we told each other about the film we'd seen over the weekend. We repeated as much as we could remember of it, word for word. I thought I had seen the film *The Picture of Dorian Grey* after Bridie told me all about it!

Bridie talked about her family: her mammy, who was blind, and her little brother, Paul, who took her mammy to the shops to get her messages. I told her every funny incident that happened in my family, like the time my brother found my sanitary towels. I had just begun buying them for myself. At last I could afford them. I had been using small pieces of old white sheets. Mammy would wash and boil them for the following month. I had my new sanitary towels in a chest of drawers in our kitchen.

"Oh I nearly died, Bridie," I whispered, "when I saw Johnny polishin' his shoes with one a'them. He had found it in the drawer and, with a finger in each loop, was swishin' it backwards and forwards cleanin' his shoes. 'They're mine,' I shouted, grabbin' them off him. 'Where did ya get them from, Lily?' he asked, as if he had discovered somethin' wonderful. 'They're smashin' for shinin' yer shoes with.'"

Bridie wiped her eyes which were wet with laughter.

"Oh, Bridie, I looked at me packet lyin' on the floor – the pads all hangin' out. I lost me temper with him and sent him flyin' out a'the way, then I gathered them up and rushed upstairs. 'You can keep *that* one,' I shouted back down to him. Now I keep them hidden in a box under my bed."

We didn't have a morning or afternoon tea break, but the older girls occasionally gathered together in the lavatory, smoking. It was a small, cold, narrow, white-washed room that stank of Jeyes Fluid. A striped roller towel hung on a wooden rail next to a chipped wash-hand basin with a rust-drip mark.

The girls tipped their ash into the sink as they hugged themselves to keep warm. They chatted, usually about one of the girls who was always sick.

"I've been goin' into the chapel, Mary, every night after work to say a prayer for her. Her mammy, Lord have mercy on her, died of the same thing – TB."

I'd wonder to myself, as I dried my hands in the wringing wet towel, why the girls would want to go to the chapel to pray on their home from work, even when it was dark and lashing rain. I thought I'd never get home for my tea and a sit by the fire. But I envied them their strong faith; it was a bond between them.

"You're a Protestant, Lily, aren't you?" one of the girls would say, picking off loose white threads from her dark tight skirt.

I'd nod.

"Well, me mammy always says that a good Protestant is equal to a bad Catholic."

They'd all look at me, as if I should be pleased.

Now and again, the forewoman would poke her head in.

"Come on, girls, you've been in there long enough," she'd remind them.

"I've got terrible pains in me stomach. I'm gettin' me granny," they'd say, holding themselves.

Then dampening their cigarettes out with their fingers and popping the butts into their skirt pockets, they'd rush out to try and catch up with their work.

Many a time a girl, rushing to get her work finished, would stop concentrating. There would be a piercing scream. A hush would descent over the factory, and a mechanic would come running out of his workshop. He'd knock off the power and try to remove the needle from the girl's finger. Often she'd faint.

Now that I was getting over two pounds a week, I managed

to save up enough money to put a down payment on a bike. As my bike was on hire-purchase, I needed a guarantor. Our milkman, Fergie, was always obliging. He went guarantee for Mammy when she bought a new cooker. Even though she was for ever falling behind with her payments and he'd be getting all the threatening letters, Fergie couldn't be angry with her. He was the sort of man that couldn't refuse anyone.

Smiling shyly, Fergie signed my form. I bought my bike from McHugh Himself in Talbot Street. It was a maroon sports-model Elswick bike. I could now cycle home for my dinner during the day.

Cycling up the hill of Prussia Street, I'd sometimes run into a herd of cattle being driven along the road to the market by cattlemen. The cattleman, in his long dirty coat and boots, would be walking behind hitting the cows with a large stick to keep them moving. I only had an hour's dinner break, so I'd have to try and cycle by. I'd look over at him, hoping he'd keep an eye on the cows near me. Pulling my bike up on to the path, I would ride by them as fast as I could.

Many times a car wanting to get by would beep its horn. The noise would frighten the cattle, and in their confusion, they'd scatter in all directions. Some would stagger up on to the narrow footpath and run blindly, their huge bodies hitting lamp-posts and anything else that got in their way. Terrified, I would drop my bike and run like mad into one of the little shops near by for safety.

"Close the door, love," a woman would call out to me from behind the counter.

I'd be late home on these days, and Mammy would be standing at the door watching for me anxiously.

"Show me! Give me your bike, Lily," she'd say, grabbing it off me at the gate.

My dinner would be on a plate over a pot of boiling water.

Annie and Johnny would be there already eating, their bikes up against the hall door ready for them to dash back to work.

"Sit down, Lily," Mammy'd say, rushing in behind me.

I would be delighted when it was my favourite: seasoned pork chop, potatoes and turnip with lots of H.P. Sauce. Mammy would fry the chop on the pan with dripping, then pour the hot brown tasty fat all over our potatoes. She'd have mashed the potatoes up with a fork and a lump of butter. Other times we'd have liver or Donnelly's Skinless Sausages', the new sausages that had just come out.

Mammy didn't know herself, now that the three of us were working. We gave her our pay packets, and she took what she needed.

In between mouthfuls of dinner, Annie chatted non-stop, while my brother sat in silence, his head down, eating his dinner. She would tell me all about two kind elderly sisters who worked with her, Bridie and Kitty. These two short, stout ladies lived together in a house on their own. They sounded so unusual.

"Kitty helps Bridie all she can, Lily," Annie would say. "You see, Bridie is older and goin' a bit blind. And poor Kitty, Lily, God help her, she even works at night sewin' away on her machine, and when her nerves get the better of her, Lily, she jumps up and plays the piano!"

"Go way!" I'd say, trying to picture Kitty banging away on her piano in the middle of the night.

As I hurried home each day, I looked forward to the next episode of Bridie and Kitty, especially the way Annie told it, filling in every detail. One day, Johnny stopped eating his dinner, put down his knife and fork, lifted his head and glared at Annie.

"I'm sick and tired," he shouted, "of ya goin' on about Bridie and Kitty. Bridie does this! Bridie does that! Kitty does this! Kitty does that! Day in, day out! I feel I'm goin' mad."

Annie and I looked at each other dumbfounded. We were completely oblivious to Johnny's presence as we chatted away. It was a long time before I heard about Bridie and Kitty again.

I loved Fridays at Burton's. We'd stop sewing early to clean and oil our machines. One of the girls would start singing, and it wouldn't be long before we'd all join in, including the men in the cutting room.

On my way home from work with my wages, I would stop at a newsagent on the quays. Leaning my bike against the wire-framed placards stacked against the shop window, I'd treat myself to a bag of mixed sweets and *Modern Romance.*

That night, I'd sit by the fire with Mammy and my sisters, reading and talking about all that had happened during the week.

I BECAME A CONVERT

Out cycling one Sunday afternoon, I met him.

"Do you live out this way?" he asked, cycling up beside me.

As we pedalled slowly along up and down the country roads around Finglas, he chatted away to me. I glanced at him. He was slightly built and looked grown up in his light-grey suit and maroon tie. He didn't tuck the bottoms of his trousers under his socks, like other boys I knew. He wore bicycle clips.

"Would you like to come to the pictures tonight?" he said suddenly. "We could go to the Bohemian in Phibsborough. I'll get tickets on my way home. I live in Fairview."

Joseph was outside the picture house when I arrived. I was a bit disappointed when I saw him off his bike. He was only

194

my height. The big Crombie overcoat didn't help; it seemed to drag him down and smother him. He smiled and handed me a box of Cadbury's chocolates, then ushered me into the cinema in front of him.

I admired his confidence, how he held his cigarette between his fingers as he talked to me, and the way he brushed his hair back from his face. And he didn't drink!

Joseph was twenty-six and had a good steady job in a bakery where his father had worked before him. He liked classical music, particularly Gigli. I loved all the romantic tunes of the forties that were being played in the dance halls around Dublin. But Joseph didn't dance, so Saturday nights we went to the pictures, and Sunday afternoons for a spin on our bikes.

When Christmas came, he made Mammy a big Christmas cake, iced with decorations. He carried it up to our house on the bus.

The following year Joseph asked me to become engaged.

"But you'll have to become a Catholic first," he said seriously.

"Why do I have to turn?" I asked him. "I am used to bein' a Protestant and like goin' to my own church."

I was worried. What would Mammy say!

"Mixed marriages never work," he said firmly. "Look at your mother's marriage. Your father's living with another woman who is a Catholic. He even goes to mass with her every Sunday. If your mother had turned Catholic, it would have been different."

I didn't like the thought of going to the same church as my father – and that other woman. I vowed to myself that if I did turn, I'd go some where else to mass, not Cabra West. *Maybe Mammy won't mind too much. She's always praising our neighbours with their strong faith, and she never turns away the chapel-girl collecting money for the new Catholic church.*

"I'm getting engaged, and Joseph wants me to turn Catholic," I told Mammy that night.

She went quiet and had to sit down.

"Well, look how you are in a mixed marriage," I added nervously.

She looked at me annoyed. "Is that what *he* said?

She sat there for a few minutes.

"Oh well, I suppose as long as you are going to some church. But, Lily, you are making a mistake in marrying him. You are not suited. He is too old and sensible for you."

Joseph wasted no time in making all the arrangements for my religious instruction. Soon I was cycling into the heart of the city to the Sisters of Charity in North William Street. I chained my bike to the railings outside the convent. Feeling nervous, I walked up the stone steps and knocked gently on the polished brass knocker. The housekeeper showed me into a small front room.

"Wait there. Mother Superior will be here in a minute," she said, pointing to a high straight-back chair.

I sat on the edge of its hard-cushioned seat anxiously and looked around. A red lamp flickered on a small table next to a statue of Mary. Holy pictures hung on the walls. The brown lino was so well polished, I could almost see myself in it. The room was cold and quiet. A horse and cart rumbled by. Life was continuing outside. The time would soon pass and I'd be outside again cycling home.

A door opened and an elderly nun appeared. She closed the door quietly and moved softly towards me. Her huge three-cornered white head-dress stood up stiffly and framed her pale, composed face. Not a blade of hair could be seen. A large brown crucifix was tied loosely around the waist of her heavy black robe. When she sat down in front of me, her robe lifted, and I caught a glimpse of her laced-up black, soft-leather shoes. She held her right hand up high.

196

"Let us begin by making a big sign of the cross. In the name of the Father, and of the Son, and of the Holy Ghost, Amen."

Her hands and nails were transparently white and spotlessly clean. She was cool, detached and never once did she smile or call me by my first name. When I was leaving, she gave me a card with the prayer "Hail Holy Queen" to learn for the following week.

Every Wednesday after work, I would go for instruction.

"The mass," she would remind me, "will flow out to you no matter where you are in the church. Now let us finish with a big sign of the cross."

The day came for my first confession.

I met Mother Superior at the convent one Saturday evening. We walked together silently along the street to St Agatha's. Her hands were tucked inside the wide sleeves of her habit. I put my scarf on my head and followed her into the church. There were rows and rows of people kneeling in front of their seats waiting for their confessions to be heard.

"Stay there," she said to me firmly.

As I stood awkwardly in the aisle of the church, she went from row to row whispering to the people that I was being converted and they were to let me go in ahead of them. Each row listened to her obediently and glanced back at me curiously.

She beckoned me down to an empty row in front of them.

"Now kneel down and ask the Blessed Virgin to help you make a good confession. Think about your sins to tell the priest."

I couldn't think of any sins he'd want to hear! Someone came out of the confessional.

"Go in now," she said quietly.

I knelt down and waited in the dark behind a tiny, closed wooden shutter. After a minute, it was flung across.

"I'm a convert, this is my first confession, and these are my sins," I said quickly.

I couldn't see the priest, only hear his whisper and feel his breath.

"Now make a good act of contrition and I'll absolve you from your sins," he said.

The next morning, I returned to be baptised and received into the Catholic Church. I thought a great mystical feeling would come over me and I would have the same faith as my friends.

But it wasn't like that.

I couldn't understand one word of the mass. The priest seemed to be miles away in this big Catholic church with his back to the people, mumbling words through a loudspeaker in Latin. Squashed behind men at the back, I felt lost. My thoughts strayed. I stared at the men's Crombie overcoats to see if the double seams were straight. A familiar damp smoky smell from their coats nearly suffocated me.

"Meet me in the city next Sunday, and we'll go to mass together," Joseph said, when I told him I couldn't follow the mass.

During the week, I mentioned to the girls at work that I had turned Catholic.

"That's great, Lily! Me mammy always says that converts can sometimes be better than Catholics."

So I still wasn't one of them – I was a convert!

The following Sunday I met Joseph in the city. We were running late. The church was packed with not one seat left. People were standing everywhere, some even sitting on the stairs leading up to the balcony where we were standing. As we were a few minutes late, Joseph insisted we stay for the whole of the next mass.

I was used to having breakfast before I went to church. Now that I had turned, I had to fast before I went to the altar.

Halfway through the second mass, I fainted. I came to as I was being carried down the stairs by a strange man. My skirt had slipped up.

"Let me down," I cried.

Standing up, I quickly fixed myself and glanced back to see Joseph rushing down the stairs carrying my hat and handbag. He looked ashamed of me. I burst out crying and pushed through the crowds of people to get outside. I was angry with him for making me stay for the second mass.

Returning home, I thought fondly of my older brother, Robbie, who was away at sea. He was still writing to Mammy and sending money. We had looked up to him like a father. I wondered what he thought about me turning Catholic. I knew Mammy had written and told him, but she didn't tell me his reply. Joseph suggested I should look for the letter. So when Mammy was out, I went upstairs to her room, knelt down and lifted the hinged lid of Granny's old black trunk. It creaked. Sylvia walked in and saw me. I didn't find the letter.

That night Mammy took me aside.

"Sylvia told me you were looking in my trunk. What were you looking for? Robbie's letter? Did Joseph put you up to that? Now he has made you deceitful and you have let him!"

I looked down at the floor and said nothing.

I was happy preparing for my marriage and our new home. We were saving hard and paying off an expensive old-fashioned dining room suite – that he had chosen.

Then one night I nearly died when Joseph told me coldly that he would not be seeing me for a while.

"In my bedroom," he explained, "there is a picture of the Sacred Heart hanging on the wall opposite my bed. When I go home at night after we have been out in the country, I kneel down to say my prayers. I look up at this picture, it condemns me, and I feel great sorrow."

I was taken aback, confused and hurt. After all I had done

for him! I missed him and fretted for weeks. Each Friday evening when I came home from work, I'd look out the window hoping he had changed his mind and I would see him sitting on his bike at the corner of our street. One evening, I cycled over to where he lived, praying he'd see me and come out.

Bridie, my pal in Burton's, persuaded me to come dancing with her again. I hadn't realised how much I had missed her, her laughter and carefree ways.

Weeks went by; then unexpectedly, Joseph reappeared and was keen to resume our relationship. I was cycling home from a dance when I saw him waiting at the corner of our street. He stopped me.

"Lily, I needed time to sort myself out with my conscience and God," he said. "I hope you understand!"

He tried to kiss me, but I pushed him away, and for the first time I noticed he had a smell off his breath.

"I'm goin' dancin' now and I don't want to go out with you any more," I said, wheeling my bike quickly towards our gate.

I gave him his ring back.

Joseph bought a car, and every Sunday morning on my way to mass in Aughrim Street he would drive slowly behind me. This went on for some time.

"He sounds a bit desperate, Lily. Be careful!" Mammy warned me.

One evening, I received a letter. I recognised Joseph's elegant handwriting and went upstairs to read it.

Dear Lily,

You have promised to marry me and in the eyes of the Catholic Church we belong together. I am responsible for your conversion into the Roman Catholic faith. If you do not consent, I will get the Catholic Church to intercede for me and they will force you.

I was puzzled and frightened. *Why does he think I belong to him under the eyes of the Catholic Church? Can he make me marry him? What if someone knocks on the door from the Church and tells me I have to?*

I came downstairs and sat in front of the fire next to Mammy. She looked at me and then at the letter in my hand.

"Lily, what are you worrying about?"

"Joseph says that the Catholic Church can make me marry him!"

"He's trying to frighten you. Don't worry, he can't force you."

I threw the letter into the fire. We both watched as the paper crumpled, burst into flames and carried on up the chimney.

A few months later, I got up the courage to go and see him. I had to know what he was doing about the furniture. Annie came with me. He kept us at the door in the rain.

"I'll leave money for you with my sister-in-law every week," he said coldly. "You can pick it up. You know where she lives in the city."

I went to her tenement room every Saturday morning.

"Sign here," she'd say in a businesslike manner, as she handed me a notebook, pen and a small amount of money.

YOU ONLY GET PAID FOR WHAT YOU DO

"Can you get me into your place?" I asked Annie one day over dinner. "I'm only getting two pounds ten a week in Burton's and I'm nearly nineteen."

"But, Lily, you can only sew straight seams. In Louie's, you're expected to make up the whole garment."

"I can sit beside you and you can show me how to do it."

"I'll try, but you'll have to let on that you're fully experienced in completing work."

I left Burton's the following Friday to work in Annie's place. Sunday night in bed, I put my head under the blankets.

Oh God, I've left me job. What am I goin' to do if I can't do the work? Burton's will never have me back, and I haven't even finished the payments on me bike yet. Oh God, help me to pick it up quick and let everyt'in' be all right.

I awoke next morning with a fright. The bed was empty. *Jesus, they're all up!*

I threw my clothes on and rushed downstairs. Annie was almost ready to go. She was standing in front of a mirror that hung over our mantelpiece in the kitchen combing her long black hair. I hurried past her into our tiny scullery where Mammy was busy brushing the crumbs off the table with her hands.

"Why didn't you call me, Mammy? I'm dead late!" I said, heading towards the sink.

"I called you several times. I thought you heard me."

I snatched a towel that was lying on the back of a chair, held a corner of it under the tap and washed my face.

"Come and sit down. I'll pour you out a cup of tea. I don't know why you're worrying about that job so much; you'll be all right."

I pulled the table out from the wall and squeezed in next to the gas stove. Reaching for my cup of tea, I dragged it across the table, shovelled in two big teaspoons of sugar and poured a drop of milk in. With both hands wrapped around the cup, I held it up to me, sipping.

"How long has this tea been made? It smells stewy."

"I'll cut you a bit a' bread. You'll need something inside you," Mammy said, holding the remains of the loaf and slicing a thick piece off.

I sat watching her frying the bread. I could see she had jumped out of bed and hadn't had time to dress. Her long black hair had fallen loose from the hairpins during the night and hung untidily around her shoulders. She had put her coat on over her nightdress to keep warm. It was unbuttoned. She looked pale and thin. I could hear Annie pumping up her bike.

"We better hurry, Lily; don't forget your scissors," she called out from the kitchen.

Still eating, I jumped up from the table, struggled into my coat and grabbed my bike. Mammy followed us.

"Wait till I help youse. I'll hold the hall door back while youse get your bikes out."

Fastening up her coat, Mammy hurried down the path after us and closed the gate. It was all hill down to the city and we cycled side by side, close to the kerb, trying to avoid the buses.

"Wait till you meet Louie, our forewoman. She runs the place. She's only young and really nice and knows all about you, Lily, turnin' Catholic. And wait till you meet Bernadette, Lily. You'll really like her. She makes all her own clothes, and when the fashion changes, do you know what she does? She rips them all up and remakes them."

Annie turned off into a side street and stopped outside a tenement house.

"What are you stoppin' here for? Where's the factory?"

"C'mon, I'll show you," she said, jumping off her bike and dragging it up on to the footpath.

We wheeled our bikes down the side of the house to a stable.

"Don't worry, our bikes will be all right here under the factory. I'll chain them together, but we'll take our pumps up with us."

"Where's the factory?" I said again, looking towards the house.

"It's just above the stable. We better hurry. I can hear them talkin' upstairs. We're the last."

With her pump under her arm, she started to climb the rickety stairs up to the factory. The sound of a door bolt being dragged back distracted me. I glanced across the yard towards an outside lavatory. The door opened and a man came slowly out still buttoning up his fly.

"He lives in the tenement. We all use the same lavatory," Annie called down to me. "Don't forget your handbag! It's still in the basket of your bike."

I ran back for my bag and hurried up the stairs after her. She pushed open a flimsy door and I slipped in behind her. My heart sank as I looked around at what Annie was calling a factory. It was a small cluttered room with only one row of old sewing machines. The machines were placed in front of two drab, dusty, rain-marked windows, which looked out towards the back of the tenement house. A group of girls who were chatting away to each other became silent and smiled over. In the far corner of the room a slim attractive woman with short brown curly hair stood in front of a table ironing. She looked over at us.

"Annie, can you help your sister get settled in, and I'll be there in a minute."

Annie nudged me.

"That's Louie!"

The power was switched on. The girls took their coats off, tied aprons around their skirts, rolled up their sleeves and sat down at their machines. I sat beside my sister. Within minutes, she was flying along on her machine, skilfully turning the material this way and that way. Straightening up for a minute, she leaned over and whispered to me.

"Get yourself a bundle of work, Lily, an' I'll show you how to do the pockets an' the fly; they're the hardest bits!"

I looked at the machine in front of me.

"I know you have an old machine, but that's all that's left!"

I gave a sigh and threw my coat over a chair behind me, grabbed a piece of rag from the floor and wiped the dust off this neglected Jones machine.

God, I wish I hadn't come! I said to myself. *Burton's was much better than here. We all had good Singer machines, our own boxes of threads and little oil cans. I'll have to search around the room for the oil can to try and do somet'in' with this bokety old machine.*

Annie looked at me concerned.

"Lily, you know it's piecework in this factory, and you'll only get paid for what you do, so you better hurry up!"

Throughout the day, the girls made up dozens of pairs of trousers with great speed. Several times Annie stopped to help me. After much sewing and ripping, I managed to complete one pair. I showed them to Annie proudly. She bit the corner of her lip.

"Oh, Lily, the pockets are crooked and the fly is too small. But here, give me them. Put them in with mine, and let's hope t'God Louie doesn't notice and passes them."

Over the next few weeks, I'd often look up and see Louie ripping up a part of my work. She'd resew it by hand, then bang it down hard with her hot iron. No matter how hard I tried, I could not earn as much money as Annie or the other girls. But my wages did increase to nearly three pounds, and I could now pay off my bike.

I wasn't there long. Due to a slack period in the clothing trade, Louie's small factory couldn't survive, and she had to let us all go.

WHERE THERE'S NO TALK, THERE'LL BE NO GOSSIP

"**G**o to Lenehans', they're looking for girls," a friend advised me.

I had been down all the back streets, in and out of poky little clothing factories, looking for work.

Lenehans' was situated in a room over a shop on the quays. It was bright and warm – unlike Louie's – with new floorboards. Ten girls were working quietly away on sewing machines. The low drone of the motors was all that could be heard.

An elderly man half sitting on the edge of a table, a cigarette hanging out of his mouth, looked up from under his glasses. He dropped what he was sewing, stuck his needle in his lapel and hurried towards me.

Is this Mr Lenehan? I wondered. This small stooped man with little bits of white thread all over his trousers, trousers that hung on him with the imprint of two bony knees showing through?

"Oh yes, I have years of experience," I lied as he took my name and address and showed me to a machine.

"My son will tell you what to do," he said, fingering his needle and thread.

I took my coat off, sat down and tried to look confident. Picking up a piece of rag from the floor, I began to clean the machine, making sure to rub off every bit of dust and grease. I reached down for my bag lying at my feet and took my scissors out. I closed my bag. The stiff metal clasp snapped sharply shut. I looked over at the other machinists. They looked away.

"How long have you been workin' here? Why's no one talkin'?" I whispered to a girl next to me.

She glanced behind me. I looked around. A tall, well-built

man with short blond hair stood looking down at me. His fresh white shirt was open at the neck, and a wide leather belt held up his well-pressed trousers.

"Are you Miss O'Shea?" he asked. "Could you please show me these trousers when you have finished them?"

With that he dropped a bundle of work on my bench and marched away. A fresh, soapy smell lingered in the air after him.

Feeling hot, I undid the buttons on my cardigan and rolled up my sleeves. My hands trembled as I threaded up the machine. Opening up the bundle of work, I laid the material across my lap, started to sew – and pray.

Oh God, he must be the son, I thought. *I don't like him much. He seems very particular about the work, not a bit like Louie. I hope these trousers are goin' to be all right. I wonder what the time is?*

After a while, when I felt it was safe, I took a quick peep to see where he was. What was he up to?

Jesus, he's right behind me standin' at that table, keepin' an eye on us while he's sortin' out orders.

He kept an eye on us all right.

"Where are you going, Miss? Please sit down!" he'd call out, whenever a girl stood up.

Jesus—we can't talk! Now we can't even move, I thought to myself.

Old Mr Lenehan could hear the girls complaining. He'd stop sewing and glare over at his son. Father and son didn't always see eye to eye in the running of the business and we'd often hear them arguing. The girls preferred old Mr Lenehan. He had worked in factories himself and understood them.

Sometimes old Mr Lenehan would bring work back to me.

"We can't pass this," he'd say, pointing to a crooked pocket. "Can I sit down beside you and show you how it ought to be done?"

Pulling a seat over, he'd squeeze in beside me. He chain-smoked and his ash would drop all over me. I'd feel embarrassed in front of the other girls, but I didn't really mind; he was teaching me how to sew the trousers properly.

I made friends with the girl sitting next to me, Kathleen. She had been working here for a long time. Whenever young Mr Lenehan had his back to us, or was arguing with his father, Kathleen and I would whisper together. She warned me about some of the girls working here.

"Watch out for that Holy Mary with the granny face opposite you. She acts all holy, going around with the black-baby box collecting for the missions. She's not to be trusted."

Kathleen was attractive with dark auburn hair. She was always last in of a morning. In she'd come, flushed from rushing, her flared skirt swishing around showing her slip. Before starting work, she'd bend her head and bless herself.

Maybe I might start doin' that, I thought to myself. *I might start swishin' my skirt and blessin' myself before I start work every mornin'.*

But I couldn't understand why she never went out at night.

"Why are you always stayin' in lookin' after your little brother?" I asked her one day.

"C'mere till I tell you somet'in', Lily," she whispered, "and, for God's sake, don't tell anyone, will ya not?" She leaned over. "He's not my little brother, he's really mine, an' I'm not married. I live at home with me mammy in Oliver Bond flats. All the neighbours t'ink he's my little brother. Mammy looks after him durin' the day. Don't tell anyone, sure ya won't!"

Sitting beside the fire that night, I told Mammy about the way young Mr Lenehan treated us.

"It's awful, Mammy, how we can't talk, and I can't understand why Kathleen doesn't mind workin' there!"

Mammy put the newspaper down and stared into the fire.

"May she feels safe in Lenehans'. Where there's no talk, there'll be no gossip!"

However, like a lot of other girls, I only stayed here for a few months. As soon as the clothing trade picked up again, I left to work in the Brunswick clothing factory.

DANCING IN THE ELITE

It was a Saturday evening. The house was quiet. Annie was gone out with her boyfriend to the Theatre Royal as usual. Sylvia and her pal who lived next door were gone to their *céilí* in St Peter's Hall, Phibsborough. Mammy was in the scullery bending over the deep stone sink washing our dirty clothes. Our big iron kettle was boiling away on the small grimy cooker. Now and again, she'd pour the hot water on top of the washing. Then she would continue rubbing the clothes hard with Lifebuoy soap. My father had dropped in and was amused watching me getting ready to go out.

"Will ya look at her, for Jaysus' sake, getting all dolled up, even painting her bloody toenails," my father called out to Mammy.

All week long I thought about nothing else, only Saturday night and dancing. And I didn't know myself now that I wasn't saving up to be married, and I could afford to buy new clothes. So when I had a few pounds saved, I would go to Cassidy's in George's Street and treat myself to a new blouse or skirt.

"Where's the scissors, Mammy?" I said, slipping my hand through my new nylons and examining the loose threads around the heels. Mammy came into the kitchen, drying her hands in her apron.

"Look in the chest of drawers, and, for God's sake, Lily, be careful! Don't go cutting a hole in your new stockings like you always do."

I snipped the loose threads, folded the stockings up carefully and left them on the back of a chair.

"That iron should be hot enough now," Mammy said, pointing to the gas stove.

Holding a bit of rag, I picked up the heavy black iron and spat on it.

"Just give it a wipe, Lily, before you iron your clean blouse and skirt."

After ironing, I heated some water up in the kettle, poured it into our enamel basin and carried it upstairs to wash myself. I came downstairs all dressed up, peeped into the kitchen and called out goodbye to Mammy.

"Enjoy yerself, love," my father shouted after me.

I had arranged to meet Bridie at the GPO.

"Have you got your lucky dress on tonight?" Bridie laughed when I met her in O'Connell Street.

Arm in arm, we hurried towards the Elite. The Elite was situated down in the basement of a well-kept Georgian house on Parnell Square. We pulled our head scarves off and made our way down the iron stairway to the entrance.

"Well, how are youse tonight, girls?" a tall, burly man at the door said, grabbing my hand and pulling me back towards him jokingly.

A loud clash of cymbals and the roll of drums sent me and Bridie rushing into the tiny cloakroom. A dance was about to begin. We gave in our coats then slipped into the hall and sat down. The band began with a quickstep to warm us up. Our hearts sank when we looked over at the row of wooden seats opposite: there weren't many boys, as usual.

"A lot will come in later after they've had a few drinks," I whispered to Bridie.

"Yes, and they'll all stand at the back and won't get up till the floor is packed," Bridie laughed.

"Oh, I love this song," I said, staring at the singer. I longed to be up dancing, but girls had to sit and wait to be asked up.

Over the weeks, I had watched the girls who sat smoking. They always looked so sure of themselves, tapping their ash on the floor and blowing the smoke out with a sigh.

"C'mon, Bridie, do you want a cigarette? I bought some on the way in."

Now, I thought to myself, *I won't care when a boy passes me by and asks the girl next to me up. I will be sittin' here smokin' my cigarette, smilin' up at the band – lettin' on I don't see him.*

I struck one match after the other, trying to light it. Then no sooner had I lit it and was puffing happily away when a boy asked me up. He stood there grinning while I tried to put it out.

But the boys didn't get it all their own way. Halfway through the night, a "ladies' choice" would be announced. Bridie and I looked forward to this dance: at last we could ask a boy up of our own choice, and they didn't like it when a girl passed them by.

I'd choose a boy who looked clean and smart, around my height or a bit taller. If the boy refused, we could report him. He would then be asked to leave. Most times, the boys readily accepted and politely returned the next dance, maybe even the next and the next.

Sometimes a group of big red-faced countrymen would come strolling into the hall. The girls would all nudge each other.

"Mother a' God, will ya look at what's come in – the culchees. They've come up for the match and forgot to go back."

The band leader would come forward and announce the next dance.

"Come on, lads, up on the floor. Don't be shy," he'd say, looking over at the boys.

But the country boys were anything but shy, especially after they had a few pints in them. Stomping across the floor, they'd grab you up to dance, hold you awkwardly and swing you around and around, lifting you right off your feet – just like they did at their *céilís*. So when we saw them heading in our direction, we'd all scatter, and if cornered, let on we didn't understand their broad country accent.

"He's askin' you up," I'd say to Bridie, trying to look serious.

"No, he's askin' you up," she'd laugh, pushing me towards him.

The country boys didn't worry too much when we refused to dance with them. They'd carry on down the row asking each girl till they found one.

We rarely refused the city boys. Wearing their best suits and shiny brogues, they'd guide you with ease around the highly polished dance floor. They'd know every dance and charm you with every song.

LIAM AND MOTHERS

In he sauntered late in the night after the pubs were closed. Feeling his eyes on me, I let on not to see him. The band announced the last dance. He quickly put his cigarette out, blew on it and popped it in his jacket pocket.

"He's comin', Lily; he's comin' down to ask you up," Bridie whispered, standing in front of me.

I kept my eyes firmly on the band – in case she'd got it wrong.

Feeling a tip on my arm, I turned around.

"Would you like to dance?" he said, pointing towards the floor.

I glanced at his light blonde hair, smoothed back, and his weather-worn freckled face. He was merry and sang every song as he shuffled me round the floor in his brown-suede, crepe-soled shoes. While we danced, I recognised his tweed sports jacket. It had been made in my factory. I told him so. His pale blue eyes laughed back at me.

"Can I see you again?" he asked as we parted outside the dance.

The following night, I caught the bus into the city to meet him. All the way in I sat and worried.

Oh God, I can't remember what he looks like, and I'm not sure that I like him. He seems a bit common. His hands are hard and rough. I wish I hadn't come. I know what I'll do. When the bus stops in O'Connell Street, I'll run across the road and get the next bus home.

The bus pulled in and I jumped off. Too late. He walked slowly towards me.

"I've got tickets for the Carlton," he said smiling. "They were booked out, but I managed to get black market tickets from a fella standing outside. He had a bundle and was selling them for twice the price."

Liam and I started going out together.

One Sunday evening he cycled over from Crumlin and suggested we go for a drink. While I was getting ready, Mammy made him a cup of tea and sat talking to him. Liam liked her and decided to give her the box of chocolates he had brought for me. When I came downstairs with my coat on, Liam stood up and looked at Mammy.

"Why don't you come with us, Missus O'Shea? We're goin'

to a small country pub. It's a nice walk through the park. Do you good to get out."

Mammy hesitated and looked at me.

"Go on put your coat on," Liam insisted.

Mammy's face lit up. She pulled off her apron, straightened her skirt and combed her hair.

"Did you see my good shoes anywhere, Lily?" she said, bending down and looking under the armchair. "I haven't been out for ages."

Liam sat there smiling at Mammy. I went over to the window, stared out and said nothing.

It was a late summer evening, and we rambled along a narrow path inside the Phoenix Park. Mammy stopped to admire the huge trees and enjoy the soft blanket of leaves that lay underneath them. She took a deep breath.

"Oh, I love that damp earthy smell," she sighed as we moved slowly on.

It wasn't long before we came to a small opening in a high stone wall that led out into a country road and to a little pub called the Hole in the Wall.

Liam bought Mammy a glass of port and fussed over her. Coming home, he took hold of Mammy's arm and linked it with his. He sang a few old songs with her quietly, while I walked out by the kerb. When we arrived home, she invited him in. My sisters were already home getting ready for bed. Mammy rushed into the scullery and put the kettle on.

"Make a few sandwiches, Lily," she called back to me. "Liam has a long way to go."

From then on, I made sure to meet him in the city.

Christmas came, and I was delighted when Liam handed me a long box wrapped in Christmas paper. Excitedly, I opened it, pulled back the tissue paper and peeped inside. My eyes lit up. A large pair of soft grey fur gloves lay snuggled there.

"They'll keep your hands nice and warm," he said smiling.

I glanced down at my hand-knitted mittens, which I wore everywhere on my bike.

How wonderful, I thought, *that he went out and chose them for me.*

I smiled to myself. I pictured him slipping into Madam Nora's, an exclusive ladies' shop in O'Connell Street. I could just see him asking the girl shyly, "Can I have those fur gloves in the window please?"

Then one night, I mentioned how much I treasured the gloves.

"My sister chose them," he answered casually.

"Your sister chose them?" I said quietly, my heart sinking.

"Yes, I gave her the money to buy you something for Christmas, and that's what she chose."

When I came home that night, I threw the gloves on the chair. The romantic, magical appeal of his choosing them for me was gone. Purely practical they were now! I wore them to work on my bike through hail, rain or sleet, not caring whether the fur got wet and mangy. And I allowed Sylvia to borrow them whenever she wished. Even Henrietta the cat was permitted to sit on them and lick them if she liked.

Liam was for ever surprising me.

"I'm taking you to a dress dance," he said one night when I met him. "You'll have to get yourself a long dress and I'll hire out a dress suit. We're going with a pal of mine and his mot."

A dress dance! I couldn't believe my ears. For years I had longed to go to one. I had often heard the older girls talking about the wonderful times they'd had at these dances. They were held in the Metropole in O'Connell Street, and you could only go with a partner. I wasted no time in going to see a dressmaker who lived on our road.

"Pink taffeta would look nice on you," she said, measuring me.

On the night of the dance Liam called for me in a taxi. He pinned a small corsage of white flowers on one side of my long pink taffeta dress.

"We're meeting John and Eileen in a pub on the quay," he whispered. "I want you to meet them before we go in."

To my relief, we didn't stay long in the pub. Liam and John stood up to leave after a couple of Guinnesses. I was dying to get to the dance. When we arrived, taxis were pulling up outside the hotel, and couples were hurrying in. So many times I had passed this hotel and envied the girls in long dresses being escorted in. Now it was my turn and I couldn't wait.

The doorman directed us to a large elegant ballroom where long tables with snow-white tablecloths were set out around the edge of the dance floor. Big white pillars stood majestically here and there near the tables. The band was playing, the lights were dimmed and couples were already on the floor. I sat in a daze, admiring the girls' dresses. Liam and I had a few dances before dinner was served. During the meal we all laughed and joked. Liam's friend, John, began to boast about his mother and the wonderful meals she used to make. Eileen joined in.

"John, d'ya remember how yer mammy used t'always do this after every meal?" she said laughing, brushing the bread crumbs off the table with her hands.

John went quiet and sat staring into space. Eileen moved her chair closer to his and put her arm around him. Liam leaned over and whispered to me, "His mammy – Lord have mercy on her – is not long dead and he's missing her terribly. She was a great mother; he was very close to her. He was the baby in the family."

We sat there saying nothing. After a few minutes, Liam left the table. The tables were cleared, the band returned, but Liam didn't!

I watched as couples were making their way on to the

dance floor, including John and Eileen. I looked around for Liam, annoyed.

Where can he be? I wondered. *Everyone is looking at me sittin' here on my own.*

I tried to smile at the couples dancing by and, for something to do, I'd stand up and fix my dress under me.

He'll be back in a minute, I reassured myself, as I tried to hide up against a pillar next to the table.

The night sailed on. All the girls were having a good time. Whenever John and Eileen weren't dancing, they'd be sitting at the table drinking and talking intimately, their arms around each other. Now and then, John would look over at me.

"Hasn't Liam come back yet?"

I went to the ladies' room many times during the night, and each time I went I hurried back praying Liam would be at the table waiting anxiously for me. Another dance was announced. The band leader came forward to the mike.

"This is a spot dance, and I want to see everyone on the floor."

Oh God, I love that dance, I cried to myself. *I wish I was up for it. I've missed all the good dances.*

I stood up. My eyes scanned the entrance.

Where in the name a' God is he?

Then rather than just sit down again, I picked up my small bag and walked slowly out of the dance hall, once more towards the ladies' room. Coming back, I took my time. It was near the end of the night and the bar was quiet. I glanced casually towards it and saw him. There he was, sitting at the far end of the bar on a stool, his blonde head down on this folded arms, fast asleep. The barman stood in front of him polishing a glass. I thought of all the times I had passed the bar during the night on my way in and out of the ladies' room. It had never entered my head

217

that he might be sitting there. Too frightened to approach him, or the bar, I rushed back and told John that I had found Liam.

"He's out in the bar asleep!" I panted.

A few minutes later Liam returned with John.

"I'm really sorry, Lily," he said, brushing his hair back with his hand. "I've spoiled your night. C'mon, let's have the last dance."

The singer came close to the mike and sang softly:

> Goodnight, sweetheart,
> Till we meet tomorrow.
> Goodnight, sweetheart,
> Sleep will banish sorrow.

Liam held me close for the slow waltz and sang along with the singer.

Coming out of the Metropole, John stumbled on the steps and fell. His loose change fell out of his pockets and scattered all around him. He lay back on the stone steps and became very emotional about his mother's death. Eileen knelt down beside him and cradled his head. I bent down to help Liam pick up John's money.

"You see, Lily," Liam said quietly, "he's been drinking heavily ever since his mammy died and he can't hold his drink."

Couples were trying to get past; some glared, looking disgusted, while others laughed. Feeling embarrassed, I straightened up and stood aside, leaving Liam to look after his friends. I was annoyed as I watched Liam hail a taxi and help them in.

If only I'd brought some money with me, I wouldn't have to wait for him to take me home.

I felt the half-crown in my hand that I had picked up on the steps and wondered if that would be enough to pay for a taxi. *If I was not wearin' this long dress, I'd be able to get a bus.* I was silent all the way home in the taxi and sat well away from him.

Next morning, I let on to Annie and Sylvia that I'd had a great time at the dance, but later on told Mammy what had really happened.

"What are you laughin' at?" I said, getting mad at her.

"Ah, Lily! Don't you see? He didn't do it on purpose. He was tired and worried about his friend. He went out to the bar and had a few drinks. The drink on top of a good feed made him fall fast asleep. He's probably feeling awful now. There's no harm in him."

One night several weeks later, I was standing at my back door with Liam. We had been for a walk and he had been quiet all evening.

"I've got somethin' to tell you," he blurted out. "I have to go to England to look for work. The textile place I worked in has closed down. There's nuttin' here for me. I don't want to go!"

We kissed and hugged goodbye and I promised to answer his letters. Suddenly, he bent down and picked up a handful of the soft black earth from our garden and cried, "I don't want to leave Mother Ireland or you."

I didn't understand when boys talked like that, calling Ireland *Mother*.

Leaning on his bike, Liam began to sob – loud, heart-rending sobs. Mammy's bedroom was just above the back door and her window was wide open. I heard her cough. I knew she was awake.

Working in Leixlip Mill

"There'll always be an England," the girls sang on our last day in the Brunswick clothing factory.

Nellie and I had both worked in the Brunswick for a year. Two weeks before our August holidays, we were knocked off due to slackness without our two weeks' holiday money. The unions were weak and had done nothing for us. At this time of the year, there was little hope of finding another job in the city. There was no unemployment benefit and we had little or no savings.

Come September, Nellie and I arranged to meet in O'Connell Street to look for work.

"'I didn't rear youse for England!'" Nellie laughed. "That's what me mammy said, Lily, when I told her I might have to go to England to work! She t'inks England is a pagan country, because me brothers have never gone to mass since they went there. And she's very worried that they might get called up."

"Well, I don't want to go to England," I said, buying a paper from a paper boy standing near by. "Come on into the GPO and we'll go through the paper, see if there's anyt'in' in it."

After several minutes of searching through the wanted ads, we found only one factory advertising for workers, and that was in Leixlip.

"Jeesus, that's miles away, Lily! How in the name a' God will we get there?

"We can go on our bikes. Let's go tomorrow. I'll call for you early," I shouted back as I ran to catch the number 22 bus.

Next morning, Mammy hurried in front of me to hold the gate open so that I could quickly wheel my bike out. She coughed for a minute trying to catch her breath.

"For God's sake, Lily, mind yourself now cycling in all that

220

mist. Just take your time, love, and I'll keep your dinner warm till you get home."

Nellie's family lived in a tenement room in Dominick Street. She was standing outside her hall door when I arrived, her bike propped up against the railings.

We chatted as we cycled along the Chapelizod Road, heading for Lucan and Leixlip. It was early and the roads weren't too busy. We cycled and cycled, watching every sign till finally we saw Leixlip. The mist had gradually lifted and a weak autumn sun had broken through.

"This must be the main street," I said, staring around. Leixlip was a quiet little town with a few small shops and a pub. "I wonder where the factory is?"

There was no one about to ask. Cars and trucks rumbled by towards Dublin.

"Here, hold me bike," I said. "I'll go into that shop and ask them where the factory is."

Looking in the window, I could see they sold everything from bundles of sticks to bread, tea and sugar. Hairpins, hairnets and shoelaces were displayed on a board. A fat tabby cat lay fast asleep next to the jars of sweets. I pushed open the door. A stout woman was behind the counter in deep conversation with a customer. Her bare red arms were folded as she leant on the counter.

"Excuse me," I interrupted, "can you tell me where the clothin' factory is?"

"Are you from Dublin?" she asked, looking me up and down. She took off her glasses and thought for a moment.

"Ah, you must be talking about the mill. I hear they've made it into a clothing factory."

She lifted up the flap of the counter, came outside and pointed up the road.

"Now, do you see that bridge up there? Well, go over it, and it's on your right, love. You can't miss it."

The mill was set well back from the road. We cycled slowly past the wild shrubs and long grass up to the entrance, then wheeled our bikes into a large, bare, cold room with tiny windows. Dust lingered in the air from the old stone floor's having just been swept. A few old bikes stood in a corner next to a roughly built open stairway. A smartly dressed man came hurrying down towards us.

"You've cycled in from Dublin!" he said, amazed.

"We had to. There's no work for us in Dublin," I explained.

"Ah, sure youse will be all right here. I've got a big order from the Irish army – uniforms and overcoats. And I'm in desperate need of experienced workers, like yerselves. I've only got ten local girls workin' here – and they're awful slow!"

We followed him carefully up the narrow wooden stairway. He paused and looked over at the empty machines.

"Ah, sit wherever youse like, girls, and listen, youse'll find everyt'in' youse need on that bench over there."

Leaving us to get settled, he went around gathering up the finished work that lay on the floor. I looked around the room. Here and there a floorboard had been replaced. The freshness of these new cream boards glared up at me in this drab, draughty factory. I shivered at the sight of the familiar khaki uniforms lying in stacks on the floor. I thought of that fella who lived next door to me. He was in the Irish army. Whenever he saw me, he'd come clumping close up behind me in his heavy army boots, shoving me out of his way, marching as if on duty.

Nellie nudged me.

"We must a' been mad comin' all out here, Lily! I don't know about you, but I'm keepin' me coat on, it's freezin'!"

"Listen, Nellie, we'll only stay here till the work picks up again in Dublin," I said, grabbing up a bit of rag and dusting down a machine.

The army uniforms weren't difficult to make, but our arms ached from lifting the heavy, coarse material.

"Jeesus, these trousers weigh a ton. They'd pull the arms out a' ya, wouldn't they?" Nellie said, rubbing her arms up and down.

"They don't seem to have much trouble," I whispered to Nellie, nodding towards the other girls.

"Yes, but they're culchees, look at the arms on them."

We worked as fast as we could, knowing we'd only get paid for what we did.

"Sure it's only the Irish army!" we'd laugh whenever we made a mistake.

The sound of seats being dragged across the floor made us look over at the other girls. They had stopped working and were now sitting close together.

"Did youse bring anyt'in' witch-youse to eat?" they called over as they munched into their thickly cut sandwiches.

I heard the rustle of paper and saw something move on the bench.

"Jesus, Mary and Joseph, there's a mouse!"

I grabbed up my lunch. Nellie shoved back her seat, bent down and stared under the machines.

"Jesus, they're everywhere," she laughed, jumping back.

"Oh my God, Nellie! Look, they've even nibbled through the butter paper to get at me bread."

The country girls stopped talking and stared over.

"Youse are not frightened of a few little mice now, are youse?" they said, grinning among themselves.

We turned our backs to them, broke off the bits of bread where the mice had nibbled and ate the rest.

As the afternoon wore on, an icy coldness came down over the mill. I spread one of the heavy army overcoats across my lap, tucking it underneath me like a blanket. This is what Mammy used to do when we'd complain that we were cold in bed; she'd throw my father's heavy overcoat over us.

At last it was six o'clock: time to go home. We hadn't seen much of the boss all day, but he was here now, turning off the power and tidying. Grabbing our bags, we made for the door.

"See youse in the mornin'," we called back to the girls as we picked our way carefully down the stairs.

Feeling tired and hungry, we had only one thing in mind and that was to get home. We cycled in and out of the puddles for miles, our lamps flickering off the dark, wet and slippery roads. My skirt kept blowing back and catching in the wheel.

"Pity we can't wear trousers like the girls in England do," I grumbled, pulling my skirt free. "Do you know what, Nellie? When Kathleen came home on holiday from the North wearin' slacks – lovely soft navy ones – men shouted after her in the street, 'Empty fly. Empty fly.' Isn't that awful!"

A bus manoeuvred around us, stopping to let people on.

"Let's get the bus tomorrow," I said. "Here, hold me bike quick before he goes. I'll go and ask the conductor where he leaves from in Dublin and I'll find out the times."

On our long journey home, we planned what bus we'd catch.

"You ride down to our house," Nellie said, "and leave yer bike on our landing."

The following morning I cycled into the city and struggled with my bike up the two flights of stairs to Nellie's door.

"Here, gimme yer bike," Nellie whispered. "It'll be all right on our landing. Me mammy is goin' to mind it for ya."

We hurried towards the quays looking for the Leixlip bus stop. The conductor was standing inside the bus talking to the driver. He flicked his cigarette butt on to the path and banged on the bell.

"Youse are just in time, girls," he laughed.

"Can ya let us know when we're near the mill in Leixlip," we panted, collapsing on a seat.

"Are youse workin' all out there?" he asked as he clicked our tickets.

The girls were already busily working when Nellie and I arrived. They looked fresh, their short hair combed and clipped back tidily from their round red cheeks.

During our lunch break, we sauntered down to the main street into a small clothes shop. A battered cardboard box lay just inside overflowing with floral aprons. I couldn't resist pulling one of these aprons out to smell the fresh new cotton. A box of colourful loose fleecy knickers lay beside the aprons. As I rummaged through them, I could hear Mammy's voice calling after me on cold mornings, "Have you got your warm fleecy knickers on, Lily? The cold will go up through you."

The hawk eyes of the woman behind the counter, who knew we were strangers, watched our every move.

"I've got some lovely pink stays for you, girls," she said, reaching under the counter and bringing up a long flat cardboard box.

The dreaded stays were supposed to hold you together and keep you warm. After a few wears of this corset-like garment, the bones poked through the flimsy cotton and its steel nose would stick in your legs as you cycled.

Nellie and I hurried out.

On our way back, we came across a narrow road partly shaded by huge chestnut trees. I kicked the golden leaves that fluttered down to a grass verge below. Bending down, I picked up one of the chestnuts and broke open the soft, prickly cone. The shiny brown chestnut lay like a baby on its white bed inside.

"I t'ink I'll bring some home to Mammy," I said, gathering them up and stuffing them into my coat pockets. "She'd love them."

Nellie joined me.

"I tell ya what, Lily! The young fellas in our house'd love them to play conkers with."

A few of the factory girls came along and were surprised to see us stuffing our good coat pockets with chestnuts. They admired the clothes we were wearing and wanted to know all about the city.

"There's great singers in the dance halls in Dublin, isn't there?"

"Are youse goin' with anyone?"

"What's he like?"

"Are youse gettin' married?"

Finally, I managed to get a word in.

"What do youse do at weekends?" I asked one of the girls.

"There's nuttin' to do here, except go for walks with the boys."

"And they take you into the fields," another girl laughed.

We all went quiet and walked back to the mill.

MY FIRST DRINK

"Do youse want a lift, girls? I'm goin' into the city," a Dublin man called out.

Nellie and I were standing at a bus stop when a van pulled up. We had just finished work in Leixlip. Feeling cold, tired and hungry, we didn't stop to think. Rushing over, we squeezed into the passenger seat beside him.

"Can youse not get a job in Dublin?" he said, flicking his cigarette butt out of his open window. "Jesus Christ, that's a terrible distance to be goin' every day. Youse must be jaded."

The bumping and rattling of the van made me feel a bit sick, and I held my head close to the open window. He stopped abruptly outside a pub, climbed out and called back to us.

"I'm goin' in for a pint. C'mon, are youse comin'? I'll buy youse a drink."

Not sure what to do, I looked at Nellie.

"C'mon, he's harmless," she said laughing, jumping out of the van after him.

As we pushed open one side of the pub door and peeped in, our van driver was standing by the bar. Catching sight of us he beckoned. We rushed over and stood next to him. Men standing close by turned and stared.

I felt strange. It didn't seem right coming into this smoky bar where there were only men. Sitting on the edge of a stool, I sipped the big glass of port put in front of me, trying to let on that I was used to it. I gazed at the bar in front of me, hypnotised by the strong lights reflecting on a large mirror. Glasses sparkled on a shelf. My head began to feel light, a warm feeling surged through me and my face looked flushed. What would Mammy say? She knew I hated drink, and I felt I was letting myself down. I tried not to think about that and chatted about our experiences in the mill – my voice getting louder.

"All the same, youse are great goin' all out there to work," our friend the van driver said.

He lifted up his glass of Guinness and emptied it. Then rubbing the back of his hand across his mouth, he picked up his cigarettes and matches and got up to go.

"Cheerio and mind yourselves now!" he said as we jumped out of the van in the city. "And don't go killin' yourselves on those army uniforms."

The street lights winked at me in O'Connell Street. The hazy rain poured down. We hurried past the queues outside

227

the Carlton towards Nellie's tenement house where I went in with her to fetch my bike. She held the door of her room open to give me some light, while I half carried it down the dark stairs and got safely out.

It was quiet on the roads at this time, not many buses. My hair felt wet and my woollen skirt was damp and beginning to rub against the insides of my bare legs. I watched couples strolling arm in arm, talking intimately – he holding the umbrella over her. Tears stung my eyes.

Goin' to the pictures, I suppose. It's not fair. I wish I could get a job back in the city. I'm fed up goin' out to Leixlip every day. By the time I get home, everyone's gone out. ~~Jesus,~~ the battery in me lamp's gone again. I hope I'm not pulled up. Mammy got such a fright last week when that policeman came to the door. That strange knock. I nearly died.

"Are you Lily O'Shea?" he had asked, in his broad country accent. We got talking and he asked me where I danced on Saturday nights. I told him and promised to meet him there and give him a dance. He tore up the fine. Mammy was listening.

"Oh, Lily, that poor chap could lose his job," she said, when I closed the door.

O, t'ank God, I'm home.

I threw my bike up against the side of our house. I could smell my dinner, which was on a large white plate over a pot of boiling water steaming away. Mammy was sitting in front of the fire in the kitchen reading the newspaper. Hearing the back door close, she jumped up and rushed into the scullery towards the cooker.

"God, you're awful late, Lily! Your dinner must be ruined. What kept you?"

She pulled up the end of her apron to grip the hot plate. My head was still feeling light and I hoped she wouldn't notice. I walked past her into the hall, took my coat off and hung it on a nail. She came hurrying into the kitchen with my dinner and put it down on the table.

"Wait! I'll pull the table over to the fire. It'll be nice and warm for you."

I dragged my chair after her.

"They've all gone out," she said, pouring me out a cup of tea.

"Have they?" I said quietly, picking at my dinner.

"Your father came round today."

"Did he! Suppose he was drunk. I'm glad I wasn't here."

"Do you know what he said?"

"What?"

"He said I looked very thin and that I should get something stronger in the chemist for my cough."

"What does he care? He's not helpin' us, is he? He comes round here whenever he feels like it, and he's growin' vegetables in his back garden. He never did that for us."

Mammy put the teapot back on the hob to keep warm, sat down and stared into the fire. After a few minutes, she stood up and brushed the bread crumbs off the table into her hands. Before throwing them into the fire, she stared at me with a worried look in her eyes.

"Have you been drinking, Lily?"

"No, I haven't!"

She went on clearing the table. I reached down for my handbag.

"I t'ink I might go to bed early," I said, getting up.

Lying in bed, I thought about Nellie, who was leaving work to get married. She was lucky; she had managed to get a small room in a tenement house in the city and planned to stay at home and have a baby. I prayed to God to help me get another job, so I wouldn't have to go to Leixlip on my own.

WE'LL HAVE TO GET SHUT OF HER

I t was Sunday afternoon. I had just come home and the house was unusually quiet.

Where's Mammy? I wondered, walking through the house towards the back door.

The lavatory door was wide open. Mammy was standing inside holding the chain, waiting for the cistern to fill up again. Her long black hair was rolled under and clipped back from her pale, thin face. A faded apron, tied at the back, hung on her. Her bare white legs were streaked with patches of red and blue from sitting too close to the fire. She was crying.

"What are you doin', Mammy?" I said, staring at the wet squirming thing in her hand.

"I've been drowning these kittens, Lily, before they get any bigger. This is the last one, thank God."

Pressing her lips tight together, Mammy pulled the chain hard. I stood beside her listening to the sharp-clunking sound as she released the chain and I watched the kitten, its eyes not open yet, disappear in the swirling water. She lifted up the bottom of her apron and wiped her eyes, then bent down and gathered up a bit of old grey blanket that had a few spots of blood on it.

"I'm not doing this any more," she sobbed. "I can't. We'll have to get shut of her!"

The trouble began soon after Henry, a smooth black cat, moved in with us. We welcomed him and gave him all our scraps of food. But Henry had one fault: he kept having kittens, one litter after the other. So Henry became Henrietta and we didn't know what to do with her kittens. It was no good offering one of them to a neighbour; they had the same problem. It was always the same, Mammy would feel terribly sorry for Henrietta after she had drowned her kittens. Bending down, she'd settle her on an old cardigan near the fire to recover.

Soon the kittens would be forgotten and Henrietta would be out again gallivanting with all the other cats in our neighbourhood. Coming home in the early morning, she'd squeeze through our kitchen window and drop to the floor, worn out. For the rest of the day, she'd curl up in our big old armchair.

One night while we were sitting quietly around the fire, we heard a soft thud in the bedroom above us.

"Shh, listen," Mammy whispered as she put down the newspaper. "What's that noise upstairs? Sounds like something's fallen off your bed."

Mammy was always worried about burglars. Neighbours' houses were for ever being broken into. Stiff with fright, we listened to the sound of someone sneaking down our stairs: flip-flop, flip-flop. The noise stopped in our tiny hall. Our eyes never left the kitchen door, waiting to see who he was. Slowly the door was pushed open and in came Henrietta, dragging Annie's large fleecy knickers behind her. After we all stopped laughing, Mammy's shocked voice went through us.

"Oh my God, she must be having more kittens."

No more was said until the following Sunday when I decided to go for a spin on my bike out into the country.

"I'm goin', Mammy," I called in, before banging the front door behind me. Mammy rushed after me.

"Listen, love. I hate asking you this, but would you mind taking the cat with you before she has any more kittens. Leave her somewhere near a farm."

Quickly lifting her up, she put her into my basket. Henrietta crouched down in the basket of my bike as I cycled out towards Finglas. I put my hand on her now and again, holding her down, and pedalled slowly along the narrow country lanes past fields full of cows and blackberry bushes.

I thought of how other people got rid of their unwanted

animals. It was quite common to see bloated sacks floating in the canals and the river Liffey. We all knew what was in those sacks. Many times I had seen a man down by the canal lift a lumpy sack off his bike and heave it into the water. My thoughts returned to Mammy. I could see her crying as she drowned the kittens. The cat had to go.

I stopped near a farm and lay my bike down gently. Henrietta crawled out and cowered up against long wild grass next to a barbed-wire fence and looked about her. I picked up my bike and cycled as fast as I could back home.

A few days later, while we were at tea, the curtain on our kitchen window began to move. A small black head peeped round the curtain, looked at Mammy and meowed, "M-a-a-a-a!"

We burst out laughing. I felt relieved. Mammy jumped up from the table and held the curtain back for Henrietta to scramble in. But it wasn't long before she had another littler of kittens.

"I can't drown them any more," Mammy sighed, staring down at the cat licking her newly born kittens. "What can we do? Can you think of anything, Lily?"

Next day, one of our neighbours stopped me in the street.

"How's yer mammy, Lily? I never see her any more, but I see yer father. He's at mass every Sunday," she said, staring into my face through her thick glasses.

Normally I'd only barely answer this woman as she loved telling me about my father. But this day, I was glad to stop.

"She's worried," I confided. "Our cat keeps having kittens and we don't know what we're going to do with them."

She put her hand on my arm, drew a deep breath and pushed back her glasses.

"Ah, Lily, for God's sake, why didn't ya ask me sooner? There's a place you can take them to. It costs ya nuttin'. It's down Blackhall Parade."

I tried to get away from her, but she kept talking to me.

"Tell yer mammy that I was askin' for her, an' tell her not to be worryin' 'bout them awld kittens, for God's sake."

I rushed in and searched round the house for something to put them all in. Rooting through an old cupboard, I found a large leather bag belonging to my father. It looked like a doctor's bag. We never knew how he came by it.

"This'll do," I called out to Mammy, turning it upside down in the grate and banging buttons and bits of fluff out of it.

I put Henrietta and the kittens into the bag and closed it. Lodging the bag sideways in the basket of my bike, I cycled like mad down the hill of Prussia Street to Blackhall Parade and the vet that was free. The veterinary was a couple of tiny rooms in a small concrete building. A few shabbily dressed men were sitting patiently on a wooden bench in the waiting room, their mangy dogs running all over the place. I stood there, the bag at my feet, and waited till the young vet with a long white coat called me in. He took the bag off me, placed it on his table, opened it up and was appalled.

"Why did you fasten that bag?" he snapped.

He lifted Henrietta and her kittens out gently on to his table.

"Didn't you realise you could've smothered them?"

Cycling home with the empty bag, I felt puzzled, embarrassed and ashamed of my life.

MY MIND'S A HELL TO ME

It was early 1952 and Mammy had stopped going out altogether. She'd send Sylvia, who wasn't working, for the messages.

"If I go," she'd say, "I'd be bound to bump into that Missus Ryan. I know I look terrible, I'm gone very thin, and she'll only start asking me questions about your father."

But my father didn't worry about the neighbours. Every Sunday he would cross our road on his way to the twelve o'clock mass, linking arms with the other woman.

Then Mammy began to have nosebleeds. I was there once when it happened.

"Hurry, Lily, put a key down my back," she shouted, holding her head back.

Frantically, I rooted around in our chest of drawers until I found our bunch of old tenement keys. They were huge, like jailer's keys, tied together with a piece of old string. In my panic, I dropped the whole bunch down her back nearly pulling her to the floor.

"~~Jesus, Mary and Joseph,~~ Lily, you nearly killed me. I didn't mean you to put the whole lot down," she said laughing, pulling the cold keys out from under her vest.

One night, when I was getting ready to go to a dance, I looked over at Mammy sitting next to the fire staring vacantly into it. Her mind was miles away. She turned and looked up at me and admired what I was wearing. I could see she was in a sad mood.

"Lily," she said, with a pleading look in her big dark eyes, "before you go out will you go to the chemist and get me a bottle of invalid port. It'll do me good, put some blood back into me."

"Oh no, Mammy, you're not goin' to start drinkin' that

stuff again are you? I hate the way you start talkin' after you've drunk it."

"Just this once, Lily, please. My mind's a hell to me, and it will help me forget for a little while."

Reluctantly, I got up on my bike and went to the chemist. Propped up against the bottles in the window was a cardboard sign: *Invalid Port For Those Who Need A Tonic.*

Mr Pelly, the chemist, took one of the bottles from his window.

Maybe it might do her good, I thought, cycling back.

When I came home late that night, Mammy was still up, sitting at the table writing one of her long letters to Robbie, who was now married and living in Queensland, Australia. A saucer of cigarette butts and ash sat next to the near-empty bottle of port. She put down her pen and with her eyes half closed lit up another Woodbine. I walked on into the scullery.

"C'mere, Lily, and sit down. I want to talk to you."

I poured myself out a glass of milk, put my newspaper of chips on my lap and sat down beside the sunken fire. I was feeling happy from my night out. Mammy looked over at me.

"Listen, Lily, when you get married, always tell your husband how you feel about him."

I knew she'd get sentimental.

"An', Lily, can you promise me something? If anything happens to me, will you look after your younger sister and brother?"

"That's why I hate buyin' you that wine, Mammy," I snapped, throwing my chip paper into the fire. "You always start talkin' like that every time you drink that stuff. I'm not gettin' it for you any more!"

I picked up my coat and went off to bed.

PADDY

"Do you see that fella down there in the navy suit and white shirt, Bridie? I'm going to ask him up for ladies' choice. You ask his friend, he's about your height. C'mon, lets go!"

His light blue eyes smiled when I approached him.

"This is the first time I've come to the Elite," he said, as he swung me around the corners. "I usually dance in the Irene."

Paddy returned the ladies' choice and every other dance for the rest of the night. I liked the way he laughed and joked. Before I rushed off to collect my coat, he caught my arm.

"Lily, would you like to come to the pictures tomorrow night? I'll try and get black market tickets."

We made a date for Sunday night.

He probably won't turn up, I said to myself. *I won't go.*

I didn't, but I thought about him all week. *Did he turn up or not?* I had to know and persuaded Bridie to come to the Irene the following Saturday.

"That's him, with the clean, shiny face and the brown brilliantined hair pushed forward into a quiff."

I watched him singing along with the band as he led the floor every dance with the best dancers in the hall. I acted surprised when he asked me up and let on I didn't remember he had told me he danced in the Irene.

"Why didn't you turn up last week?" he said angrily. "I stood in the freezing cold sleet waiting for you for over an hour!"

"I didn't think you'd turn up," I said, looking all surprised. But I was flattered that he had. We made another date. This time he let me down.

I dragged Bridie back to the Irene. As usual, Paddy was

leading the floor for every dance. I let on not to see him and danced with other boys. He waited till the last waltz before he came looking for me. I was standing in a crowd at the back. Gripping my arm, he led me firmly out of the smoky atmosphere on to the dance floor.

"Sorry for not turnin' up last week," he said. "I saw you waitin'. But you let me down the previous week, and I wanted to let you know what it felt like."

So he really does like me!

"Will you give me another chance? Let's meet next Saturday night. I promise you, I'll be there."

I hesitated. Putting his hand inside his jacket he pulled out his wallet.

"Here take this. Now do you believe me?"

He was standing outside Findlaters' shop the following week when I arrived with his wallet. His face lit up when he saw me. Taking my arm he guided me in to the Maple Leaf Café close by. We took off our coats and laid them on the seats beside us.

"Egg and chips for two, please, bread and butter, and a big pot of tea," Paddy said, smiling to the waitress.

It's nice here, I thought, *sitting in this alcove, all on our own.*

He told me all about himself.

"I just live round the corner, Lily, in Gardiner Street with my mother and three brothers. There were nine of us; the rest are married."

He chatted about the Irene and the girls he danced with every week.

"One of the girls I dance with got me a job in Irish Textiles as a knitter," he said, pleased with himself.

I looked around.

"But we are just friends," he quickly added.

In the privacy of the alcove, I found myself telling him that I had once been a Protestant like Mammy.

"Why did you turn?"

"Because I was engaged to a Catholic boy. He insisted I become a convert."

I waited for his reaction.

"That must have been hard on your mother, Lily. I'm a Catholic, but it wouldn't have made any difference to me."

I was glad he wasn't holy like Joseph.

There was a jukebox on the wall beside us.

"Let's play a tune before we go," I said, changing the subject.

From then on, Paddy and I would meet every Saturday evening outside the Maple Leaf. After tea we'd stand, arm in arm, in long cinema queues, sometimes for hours in the pouring rain. He would hold my red umbrella over both of us, and we'd chat about everything we had done all week. I enjoyed the buskers singing and playing their accordions as they walked up and down the queue. But Paddy was impatient, and whenever the doorman came out and shouted "single seats only" he'd rush to get them.

"C'mon," he'd say, "once inside we can watch out for seats together."

In the 1950s films were repeated over and over, and people would often arrive after the film had started and leave before it finished.

The national anthem was always played at the end of the night. The lights would go on and everyone would stand to attention like statues. Whenever I went to the pictures with Bridie we were too frightened to squeeze by others to get out. Some little man would invariably give us a dig and a bull's look. We would have to wait till they finished singing "Fianna, Fianna Fáil". They didn't care that we might have a bus to catch.

But with Paddy it was different. He wasted no time. As soon as the film ended, he'd nudge me and whisper, "Quick, grab your coat and bag; let's try and dodge out before the anthem."

I was glad Paddy wasn't real patriotic like Liam.

We'd hurry for the 22 bus to Cabra West, get off at the terminus and buy some chips. I'd help Paddy eat his as we sauntered down Killala Road to our corner. We'd stand for a while in the dark. My small bag of chips would be keeping warm in one of my fur gloves, the ones Liam bought me. I'd have my chips later with a glass of milk when I went in.

MAMMY TAKES TO HER BED

Coming home from work one warm spring evening, I opened our gate and saw Mammy sitting on the doorstep, a cushion under her. She was hidden from view by a high hedge in front of our garden. I noticed how pale and frail she looked.

"Hello, Lily, I'm letting some heat get into my bones," she said cheerfully.

"Mammy, why don't we look for a doctor for you?" I said, when I saw her struggling to get up.

"No, I'll be all right. It's all to do with my old trouble, the operation I had years ago. Besides we can't afford it."

"Look," I said, "the Whit weekend is comin' up. I'll be off work. You can stay in bed and have a good rest. I'll look after you."

"Okay, Lily, I'll do that."

During the Whit weekend, I tried to nourish her back to health. I ran up and down the stairs with her meals and egg flips – she always gave us egg flips when we were run down.

239

"You look tired," Mammy said when I gave her her dinner on Monday.

As I turned to go downstairs, the room spun. I reached for the wall and sank slowly to the floor. When I came to, my father was helping me up. I could hear Mammy's anxious voice.

"Thank God you dropped in, John. She's been looking after me all weekend. I don't think she's eating anything herself. I better get up."

She pulled her blankets back to get out of bed.

"No, Mammy, stay there," I called over.

"Come on, love," my father said, supporting me down the stairs.

I sat in a daze as he busied himself in our scullery.

"Here, love, get this down ya an' ya'll be fine," he said, handing me a bowl of thick porridge.

I ate every bit of it – amazed he could make it. He was a bit jittery and kept glancing out of the window.

I suppose he's worried your woman might be home.

I wanted to talk to him about Mammy, but he was not the kind of man you could have a serious conversation with. He didn't seem to know how to, not like Paddy.

"I'll have to go now. Mind yerself!" he said, snatching his jacket off the back of the chair and rushing out.

Mammy was no better after the weekend, and my sisters and I encouraged her to stay on in bed, hoping she'd get well. From her bed she organised all the jobs around the house. Sylvia swept the floor and cooked the dinner. She had great pride in the house and was for ever Brassoing our letter box, while she chatted to her pal. We had the shiniest letter box on Drumcliffe Road. And I was still the only one who was allowed to clean out the grate. No cinders in our bin! And I made sure every grain of sugar was shaken out of its bag. Annie was great at getting a bargain, and Mammy praised her no end, but sometimes Annie got carried away.

When she left home to get married, Sylvia and I found a pile of brand new shoes under our bed that didn't fit any of us, but they were all good bargains.

Two months went by and Mammy was still in bed. She rarely saw anyone but us, so I was glad when one Sunday morning a neighbour's daughter knocked on our door.

"Lily, can I show yer mammy me new baby?" Susie said proudly.

I led her upstairs. Mammy's face beamed when Susie gave her the baby to hold.

Miss Snow was Mammy's only other visitor. This tall, thin, straight-backed Protestant lady devoted her time to the sick of her parish, All Saints. I never knew when to expect her and would go into a panic when I'd see her coming down our road.

"Oh my God, here's Miss Snow!" I'd say, rushing up the stairs to tidy Mammy's room.

"I've come to see your mother," Miss Snow would smile when I opened the hall door.

I'd hold the door back and she'd go straight upstairs. After a few minutes, she'd tiptoe back down.

"Could I please have a basin of warm water, soap and a towel?" she'd ask in her gentle voice.

I would shove our big iron kettle on the gas cooker to heat up some water and look around for a clean towel. I was grateful to Miss Snow and admired her. I couldn't wash Mammy all over like she was doing. When she was finished, she'd come back down, hand me the basin and, without saying one word, open the hall door and go. I'd empty the basin and run up to hear what Miss Snow had had to say. Mammy would be sitting up looking refreshed in her clean night-gown with the bedclothes neatly tucked in.

"I feel grand now after that wash, and do you know what Miss Snow always says, Lily?"

"What?"

"Don't worry about your children, they'll eventually come back to their own religion."

Annie was engaged to a Catholic boy and had also converted.

"I hope she didn't see the po under your bed," I said, changing the subject.

As our lavatory was outside our back door, we kept a white enamel po upstairs during the night. It was now permanently under Mammy's bed. Every night I would wake up to hear her coughing as she called out to me.

"Lily! Lily! Lily!"

Half asleep, I'd drag myself out of bed to give her the po.

"I'm sorry, love, for getting you up this hour of the night. Now run back before you get your end of cold."

I'd put newspaper over the po and shove it back under her bed. My sisters would grumble when I'd crawl back into bed and curl up behind them.

My father began coming around more often, sometimes carrying a big bowl of hot vegetable soup. He'd sit on the edge of Mammy's bed and spoon-feed her.

"This'll do ya good. I made it meself," he'd say proudly.

I would hang around the bedroom, watching him suspiciously as he washed Mammy's hands and face with a wet corner of her towel.

"Go on out, Lily, and see Paddy. I'm all right, honestly," Mammy would say, seeing my worried face. I hadn't forgotten the day when I came home and found Mammy very distressed.

"While youse were out," she told Annie and me quietly, "your father came round and forced me upstairs. He made me go up because he said I'm still married to him!"

But my father seemed to be genuinely concerned for her now.

Johnny and I saved up and bought a small record player between us. Whenever I'd buy a new record, I'd play it over and over. Opening the kitchen door, I'd turn the volume up, so that Mammy could hear it. I went up to her room once to see how she was enjoying it. She was lying back on her pillow, looking exhausted.

"Lily, will you please close the kitchen door. I don't really want to hear Mario Lanza singing 'Be My Love' any more."

August came, and Annie was getting married. Before we left for the church, she ran up to Mammy in her long white wedding dress. When Mammy saw her, she broke down and cried. It was a small, quiet wedding. My father gave Annie away, while Mammy stayed home in bed alone.

MAMMY DIES

"I haven't got enough breath to talk, Lily; my chest is hurting me," Mammy said one night.

Worried and upset, I went to a neighbour and asked her if she knew of a doctor.

"There's one on the Navan Road, Lily, if you want to get him. He lives in a private house."

When Dr Kirwan came he sounded her chest and, without saying one word to Mammy, walked abruptly out of the room. He turned to me on the stairs.

"Why in the name of God didn't you get me before now? You wouldn't let a dog die like that!"

"She wouldn't let me!" I said, feeling terribly ashamed.

He didn't answer me, but stood for a minute at the hall door staring back up the stairs towards Mammy's room.

"Look, I'm going to send her for x-rays anyway. An ambulance will come tomorrow and take her to the hospital and back home again."

After Mammy had the x-rays, I went to see Dr Kirwan for the results. He brought me into his surgery.

"Your mammy's lungs are riddled with TB. There's not much hope. However, I will still have her admitted to hospital and we'll do all we can."

It was only then I realised the seriousness of Mammy's illness. I was for ever hearing about someone in work being admitted into one of the overcrowded sanatoriums around Dublin. I thought about the Cafferty family, who had lived in the corner house on our block. The whole family died of TB within one year. First the father, six months later the mother, and then the two grown-up girls, Kathleen and Mary. That was over a year ago and their house still stood empty except for their furniture, which had never been claimed.

My father came immediately when he heard the news. When I opened the hall door, he rushed past me up the stairs, and gathering Mammy up in his arms, he kissed her lovingly.

"Dolly is dyin'! Doll is dyin'!" he sobbed, stumbling back down the stairs.

I was furious with him. I had made sure not to tell Mammy what Dr Kirwan had said. I let her believe she was going to get better. I stood at the end of the stairs and held the hall door wide open for him to leave. When I went back up to Mammy, she was quiet and did not let on to me that she had heard.

The word got around with the neighbours, and they would stop me in the street and touch my arm.

"How's yer poor mammy, Lily? God love her."

Our neighbour, Mrs O'Connell, who lived directly opposite our house, came over and knocked on our door. She stood there with her arms tucked inside the front of her apron.

"Lily, can I see your mammy before she goes to hospital?" she asked me in a sympathetic voice.

I liked Mrs O'Connell. I knew that she herself had not had an easy life with her husband. Mammy's face lit up when she saw her. She struggled to sit up. Mrs O'Connell rushed towards Mammy with her arms outstretched. Frightened that she would hurt Mammy, I quickly stood in front of her.

"Leave her, Lily," Mammy wheezed. "I need to be held."

I stood back puzzled. *Why does she want this neighbour to hold her?* This was something we didn't do.

Mrs O'Connell held Mammy in her arms without saying one word, for what seemed to me a long time.

A few days later, Dr Kirwan called around and told me he had arranged for Mammy to be admitted into hospital the following Monday, 13 October. The night before she was to go, I sat on the edge of her bed reassuring her that she would be all right once she went into hospital. She lay back on her pillow, holding her chest, barely able to speak.

"I just hope they can give me something to help me breath easier."

I hurried down to Dr Kirwan and told him she was finding it hard to breathe.

"This will help her have a good night's rest," he said, handing me some tablets.

I got up early the next morning and went into Mammy's room. I don't know why, but for the first time I noticed the room. It was a tiny room with cream-distemper walls. A dark blue velvet mat that Robbie had sent her lay on the bare wooden boards next to her single iron-framed bed. Floral curtains drooped from a wire at the window. A kitchen chair stood next to the bed with her glass of water. There was something else on this chair, the only bright thing in this drab room. It was a small glass-domed ornament filled with water and a country snow scene. Annie had brought it back for Mammy from her honeymoon.

"Mammy, wake up," I said, touching her.

"I only want a cup of tea," she said drowsily.

When I brought her up the cup of tea, she opened her eyes but made no attempt to sit up. So I put the cup and saucer on the chair, sat her up against the pillows and held the cup of milky tea up to her. She could not swallow and it dribbled out of the corners of her mouth. She was silently wheezing. I placed the cup back down on the saucer. I didn't know what to do. I walked over to her window and pulled back the curtains. A heavy mist was falling on our overgrown back garden. Tears streamed down my face. I looked back at her. She was watching me with a concerned look in her big eyes.

"What's wrong with you, Mammy? Why are you not drinkin' your tea?" I cried, walking back towards her.

I sat down on the edge of the bed, my hand resting on the covers near her.

"Mammy, the ambulance will be here at ten o'clock. I've got to get you ready."

She lifted her hand and put it over mine very gently, as if the say, *It's all right, Lily, don't worry.*

Her eyes closed.

I heard the hall door open downstairs. Sylvia was talking quietly to someone. I rushed down. It was Annie. She had come over hoping to see Mammy before the ambulance arrived. We stood talking quietly.

"What's that noise?" I said, staring up towards Mammy's room.

Annie and Sylvia looked at me helplessly. I dashed back up to Mammy's room, then ran down out into the street and banged off my neighbour's door.

"Missus Cullen! Missus Cullen!" I shouted, "there's something wrong with Mammy. She's making a strange noise, a gurgling noise."

Mrs Cullen was a tough Dublin woman. She was always standing at her hall door, watching everyone and everything that went on in our street. I don't know why I turned to her that morning.

Mrs Cullen quickly wiped her hands in her apron.

"I won't be long. I'm goin' next door to O'Sheas'," she called back to her children.

She rushed after me up the stairs past my sisters, who were still standing at the hall door looking shocked. The noise was louder.

"That's the death rattle, Lily," Mrs Cullen said. "I'm afraid yer mammy's dyin'."

Taking over completely, she bent over Mammy, muttering a prayer, constantly making the sign of the cross over Mammy's mouth.

"Quick, Lily, ya have to help me. Get me yer headscarf. Now hold yer mammy's chin up while I tie the scarf."

I didn't have time to think about what I was doing. Mammy's face felt lukewarm. She seemed to be asleep.

"Get me a basin of water, flannel, towel and clean sheets. I'm going to wash yer mammy."

I gave her everything she wanted.

"Now ya get out, Lily. I don' t want ya in here."

She pushed me out on to the landing where I stood outside the door. Eventually she came out and handed me Mammy's wedding ring.

"That ring now goes to yer eldest brother, and if ya can't contact him it goes to yer youngest brother."

I didn't want the ring taken off Mammy's finger. That was the one thing that she would never remove through all her hard years. But by this time I was very confused and didn't know what was right any more. I walked slowly back into the bedroom where my neighbour had drawn the curtains. The room was dim and smelt of Lifebuoy soap. I stood just inside the door and forced myself to look over at Mammy's bed. She was lying flat on her back. Mrs Cullen had dragged Mammy's hair back so severely it didn't look like her at all. It was strange not to hear her coughing any more. Mrs Cullen came back upstairs after emptying the basin, wiping her hands in her apron. She grabbed hold of me by the shoulders.

"Now, Lily, listen to me! Go down and get yer mother's minister and when he comes up to the house ask him for the money for a habit for yer mammy so that she can be laid out properly. I have to go now to get the children's dinner. Call me again if you want me. Don't t'ank me, Lily, I'll get me reward in heaven. Yes, I'll be rewarded in heaven."

I came downstairs and walked into the scullery. My two sisters followed in behind me.

"I'll make us a cup a' tea," Annie said, filling up our iron kettle.

A strip of wallpaper hung down over our cooker where the constant steam from our kettle, pots and pans had made it loose. It had been like this for a long time, and cobwebs had gathered underneath it. I hadn't worried too much about it before, but now it annoyed me. I rooted around in the cutlery drawer searching for a box of thumbtacks. I dragged the table over to the cooker, climbed up on it and tacked up the paper. With an old rag, I began to clean the greasy, dusty shelf above the cooker. My sisters stood staring up at me.

The word got around the neighbours that Mammy had died. Every curtain was pulled immediately and would remain so until after the funeral. People glanced in as they walked softly by.

The clergyman came that afternoon. I led him up to

Mammy's room, where he knelt down and said some prayers. Coming down the stairs, I told him what my neighbour had said. He answered me abruptly.

"We Protestants do not wear habits like the Catholics do. You buy your mother a new nightdress. That's all that'll be necessary."

And then without a word of comfort, he was gone.

That evening Annie went home to her husband and Sylvia went to stay with her pal. Paddy invited me to stay overnight in Gardiner Street with his family.

"You can climb in behind my mother in her big feather bed," he said, trying to comfort me.

I sat in front of his mother's range shivering. I was wearing a long, heavy, brown flared skirt. I wrapped this skirt around my legs, hugging my knees. I felt cold and numb inside. Paddy's mother, a big friendly woman, fussed over me, making me tea and poking the range to get more heat. Paddy and his brothers sat quietly watching me.

"Lily, I would've washed yer mammy for ya," his mother said kindly, "an' so would've our Lizzie. She would've done it too, Lily. She lives on Killala Road around the corner from ya if you need her."

I felt awful about Johnny. He was sleeping in our house all on his own.

"Mammy is lyin' dead in the room next to his," I said, looking at Paddy's mother.

"Ah, I wouldn't worry, Lily. He'll be all right. The dead wouldn't harm ya. It's the livin' ya have to be mindin', not the dead!"

Mammy had made sure to keep up to date with her death insurance, but as my father was still married to her up to the time of her death, the insurance company insisted he should be given the funeral money. My father came around with the funeral papers. He showed them to me.

"Glasnevin! That's a Catholic cemetery! Mammy is a Protestant and should be buried in Mount Jerome where Granny is buried."

I held on to the papers and told him I was going back down to Farrell's, the undertakers in Marlborough Street, to have them changed. He looked at me angrily.

"All me married life to your mother I never got me own way, an' now, not even after her death!"

On the day of the funeral my sister, Kathleen, who was married and living in England, sent flowers. A letter came for Mammy from Robbie – the letter she had been waiting for. My father came to the funeral wearing his best suit and a black tie.

A group of our neighbours came to the church to show their respect but stood outside the church door. As Paddy and my closest friend, Nora, approached the church with me, the neighbours stepped forward and warned them.

"Don't go in there! Youse are Catholics. If youse go inside that Protestant church, you'll be committin' a mortal sin."

Paddy and Nora ignored them and followed me inside. But the neighbours did enter Mount Jerome cemetery, though they stayed a good distance away from the grave and the clergyman's prayers.

Back in work, all in black, I was approached by the foreman, who said how sorry he was.

"What did yer mammy die of, Lily?" he asked me sympathetically.

Not wanting to appear poor, I couldn't say TB.

"Her lungs," I answered quietly.

He nodded understandingly and walked away.

A week later, a van pulled up outside our house from the Dublin Health Department. Several men in uniforms jumped out and banged off our door and, without explaining anything, they rushed ahead of me upstairs.

"What bed did the person die on?" the men demanded.

They pulled Mammy's mattress off the bed springs, fumigated it, then left it lying there damp, sagging against the wall.

Within the week a letter came from the Health Department, insisting that we all attend an x-ray clinic immediately.

Johnny refused to go. Sylvia and Annie's x-rays were clear. Mine showed a small scar on my left lung. The first sign of tuberculosis.

I was summoned back to the hospital for TB tests.

"Cough into that," a big country nurse demanded as she shoved a small white-enamel bowl in front of me.

I tried my best to cough and please this nurse, but couldn't.

"Try harder," she shouted over and over again.

To my relief, I was told that the scar was not active, and I was to look after myself.

I hurried off home, up Blackhall Parade, dying to tell Mammy the results. I had forgotten she was gone!

We carried on as Mammy would have wanted. Sylvia got the messages and cooked our dinner during the week, while Johnny and I went back to work. But the house had a terrible loneliness about it. I hated going upstairs, it was so quiet. The familiar sound of Mammy's coughing had been comforting.

The weekends were the worst. I'd creep around the house in my black jumper and skirt. Wearing black, I thought I had to be sad and felt guilty if I laughed or joked. I would take out the pink twinset, the cardigan and jumper that Paddy had bought me for Christmas, try it on, then put it back in its box again. It didn't seem right to wear it, not just yet. And I couldn't play a record or go to the pictures. What would the neighbours say?

"Ya need a neighbour, Lily," Paddy's mother would remind me. And I knew she was right. What would I have done without them? But I felt their eyes on me all the time. Whenever

I'd open the door to Paddy, I'd see a neighbour's curtain move and then drop. But what would I have done without *him* and his happy, easygoing nature?

One Sunday afternoon I was tidying up the kitchen, brushing the crumbs off the table and sweeping them into the coal-hole. I wanted the place to look clean. Paddy was coming up for tea. Sylvia was next door with her pal. Johnny was sitting on a kitchen chair in front of the fire, lost in his thoughts, one foot on each side of the fender.

"God, isn't it awful cold?" I said, rubbing my arms up and down.

"That's funny, I don't feel it," Johnny mumbled without looking around.

"That's because you're sittin' on top of it," I snapped.

Startled, he glanced up at me and then roared with laughter.

"I'll build up the fire to make the place cheerful," he said, grabbing the empty coal bucket and shovel.

As he walked towards the coal-hole, he held the shovel out as if to scoop me up.

"Oh sorry, Lily! I thought ya were a bit a' black coal walkin' around."

I burst out laughing.

Acknowledgments

Writing demands time, time I could have spent with my family and six grandchildren. So my thanks to them for their understanding and encouragement over these last few years. I think of my book as a gift to them.

I am grateful to my son, Steven, who first put the idea into my head that I had something of value to say. As a young boy, he showed great interest in my past and constantly encouraged me to write it down. Niall Brennan, an Australian writer, further kindled this idea by reminding me that "though other Irish experiences have been written, *yours* hasn't." Thanks Niall.

And I would like to thank Mimi Roennfeldt for her encouragement and support, and her attentive care in checking my grammar without changing my voice.

I am deeply indebted to David Norris for his confidence in me, and his interest in the times I was writing about.

And what would I have done without Bryan's help, my other son? Our endless discussions on my writing were invaluable to me, and his long labouring hours helping me on the computer were a credit to his patience.

Finally, I'd like to thank Brandon for their careful reading of my manuscript and positive suggestions.

FICTION
from
BRANDON

KITTY FITZGERALD
Snapdragons

"A unique and extremely engaging story of two sisters, each of whom is looking for love and salvation in their different ways." *Irish Post*

"An original, daring book." *Books Ireland*

Sometimes shocking, frequently humorous, often surreal, *Snapdragons* is a unique and extremely engaging rites of passage novel about a young woman who grows up unhappily in rural Ireland after World War II. She is disliked – for reasons she cannot understand – by her parents, and has a running feud with her sister. Yet the mood of this story is strangely light-hearted, frequently comic and absolutely memorable.

She makes her escape to the English midlands, and works and lives in a pub in Digbeth, Birmingham, where her sister has settled with her husband. Her already difficult relationship with her sister is further strained when she discovers how she is living. She also learns the sad reason for her parents' hostility towards her.

A captivating story of a young girl in Birmingham and the North of England in the 1950s, its main protagonist, Bernadette, who carries on a constant angry dialogue with God, is one of the most delightfully drawn characters in recent Irish fiction.

ISBN 0 86322 258 7; Original Paperback £8.99

JOHN TROLAN

Slow Punctures

"Compelling. . . his writing, with its mix of brutal social realism, irony and humour, reads like a cross between Roddy Doyle and Irvine Welsh." *Sunday Independent*

"Three hundred manic, readable pages. . . *Slow Punctures* is grim, funny and bawdy in equal measure." *The Irish Times*

"Fast-moving and hilarious in the tradition of Roddy Doyle." *Sunday Business Post*

"Trolan writes in a crisp and consistent style. He handles the delicate subject of young suicide with a sensitive practicality and complete lack of sentiment. His novel is a brittle working-class rites of passage that tells a story about Dublin that probably should have been told a long time ago." *Irish Post*

ISBN 0 86322 252 8; Original Paperback £8.99

Any Other Time

It's 1986, Dublin. Meet Davy Bleedin' Byrne. Hardworking, enterprising, and full of initiative, Davy is a sign of the time. Dribbling at the brim with intent, and with the reluctant support of his buddy Mickey Hughes, Davy doesn't take what he thinks should be his, he takes what he wants. The consequences are comical, disastrous and tragic.

Any Other Time evokes a time and a place with startling immediacy. Set in the underworld of junkie Dublin and refreshingly written from the inside out, it conveys the inescapable feeling that nothing has been omitted, besides the numbers on the doors.

ISBN 0 86322 265 X; Original Paperback £8.99